ML

UNIVERSITY OF STRATHCLYDE

30125 00443780 1

D1585285

ANDERSONIAN LIBRARY
✶
WITHDRAWN
FROM
LIBRARY
STOCK
✦
UNIVERSITY OF STRATHCLYDE

Books are to be

33

uStrath

Marketing by Matrix

#25758195

MARKETING BY MATRIX

100 Practical Ways to Improve Your Strategic and Tactical Marketing

Malcolm H. B. McDonald

AND

John W. Leppard

Butterworth-Heinemann Ltd
Linacre House, Jordan Hill, Oxford OX2 8DP

 PART OF REED INTERNATIONAL BOOKS

OXFORD   LONDON   BOSTON
MUNICH   NEW DELHI   SINGAPORE   SYDNEY
TOKYO   TORONTO   WELLINGTON

First published 1992

© Malcolm H. B. McDonald and John W. Leppard 1992

All rights reserved. No part of this publication
may be reproduced in any material form (including
photocopying or storing in any medium by electronic
means and whether or not transiently or incidentally
to some other use of this publication) without the
written permission of the copyright holder except in
accordance with the provisions of the Copyright,
Designs and Patents Act 1988 or under the terms of a
licence issued by the Copyright Licensing Agency Ltd,
90 Tottenham Court Road, London, England W1P 9HE.
Applications for the copyright holder's written permission
to reproduce any part of this publication should be addressed
to the publishers

British Library Cataloguing in Publication Data
McDonald, M. H. B. (Malcolm H. B.)
  Marketing by matrix.
  I. Title   II. Leppard, John
  658.8

ISBN 0 7506 0408 5

Photoset by Redwood Press Limited, Melksham, Wiltshire
Printed and bound in Great Britain by
Thomson Litho Ltd, East Kilbride, Scotland

UNIVERSITY OF STRATHCLYDE
-9 JUN 1993
UNIVERSITY LIBRARY

D
658.8
MACD

Contents

Introduction

Marketing is a delightfully simple concept to talk about, yet, as any marketers will tell you, it is far from easy to put into practice.

There are many different reasons for this, and here are just a few of them. No doubt you will think of others as you read down this list.

- Marketing is ill-understood in the organization.
- There is no marketing plan.
- There is no 'plan' for planning.
- The corporate culture is not marketing orientated.
- Not enough resources are allocated to marketing.
- Not enough information of the right sort exists about customers, products, competitors, trends and so on.
- Roles that people are expected to play are ill-defined, misunderstood or confusing.
- There is a lack of clarity about where the organization is going and what it wants to achieve.

Indeed, it was to address many of these issues that an earlier book in this series was written by one of the authors.*

However, we believe that there is another problem which besets marketers and their colleagues at work. This is to do with the fact that to alter one element of marketing automatically has an impact on another. Thus, the inter-relationships between many factors have to be taken into account. For example, there is generally a fairly obvious relationship between the price charged for a product or service and the volume of sales which result.

Equally, one might expect the uniqueness of a product and the sort of people to whom it might appeal to be related in some way.

Therefore, the marketer is not dealing with certainties, but with possibilities. He or she is striving to find answers to problems embracing a range of multi-dimensional variables.

Our experience of working with companies on marketing-related problems has led us to believe that frequently the organization is applying 'one dimensional thinking' to what are clearly multi-faceted problems. In these circumstances, we have found that the use of 'two dimensional' thinking can often help to simplify a complex situation and help to clarify the relationships.

We accept that the purists among our readers might comment that the matrices we have included here are an over-simplification of complex problems. We would not argue with them on this issue, because intellectually there is much truth in what they say. Nevertheless, when practical decisions are required in a hard and competitive world, any 'tools' which lead to higher quality outputs are not to be spurned lightly.

Of course, the idea of bi-polar diagrams, or matrices as we've chosen to call them, is not new. Many of the influential breakthroughs in marketing in recent years have used this format. *What is new* is that we have assembled some of these 'classic' matrices, and added many others we have developed and used ourselves. They are presented in this book, with full explanations, grouped under a number of different headings for easy reference.

* McDonald M. H. B., *Marketing Plans* (Butterworth-Heinemann, Oxford 1989).

How to use this book

The intention behind this book is that it should be used as a reference, to prompt ideas or new avenues of thought. It certainly isn't the sort of book where one starts at the beginning and reads through to the end.

We believe that many marketers, be they experienced or students, will find much of interest in these pages. Moreover, we hope that readers will be stimulated to develop matrices for their own situations and as a result, win success.

There could be no better testament for this book than if they were to do this.

© *Malcolm H. B. McDonald, John W. Leppard*
Cranfield, June 1991

1 General strategic issues

1 Company strategy and tactics

A successful company needs to get both its strategy and operations (tactics) working effectively. This matrix illustrates dramatically just how important it is for a company to 'get its act together'.

	Strategy	
	Ineffective	Effective
Efficient	Die (quickly) 3	Thrive 2
Inefficient	Die (slowly) 4	Survive 1

(Tactics on vertical axis)

Box 1 Good effective strategy, but inefficient tactics – a recoverable situation by moving vertically upwards.

Box 2 The best possible situation – an effective strategy combined with efficient operations.

Box 3 The wrong strategy, efficiently implemented! Surely the way to a quick death!

Box 4 The wrong strategy, inefficiently implemented – in this case a long, slow, lingering death!

Note:

The vertical axis, *tactics*, is often mistaken to be what management is all about. As long as you go faster and are seen to be active, all is well. We call this the *superman* or *wonderwoman syndrome*!

Ratio management is a key measure of such behaviour (i.e. sales costs divided by revenue, or advertising costs divided by revenue). The model in their tiny minds, however, is that salespeople and advertising are *caused by sales*! Cut out *all* costs and see what happens to profits! A company doing this would be the most profitable company in the world . . . for a day, perhaps!

2   Strategy and tactics time allocation

Matrix 1, looked at how strategy and tactics both needed to be effectively managed. This matrix goes on to examine the vexed issue of time management. Just how should managerial time be allocated to strategic and operational matters?

Manager orientation

	Strategy	Tactics
Board	4	3
Operations	1	2

Level of seniority

Box 1   People in this box generally cause organizations to go bankrupt! They are operational people, yet their orientation towards tactics/operations is low. Such people rarely actually do anything. Instead, they spend most of their time saying how the company should be run.

Box 2   People here should obviously spend the majority of their time implementing policy – in other words, *doing things*! However, some of their time should be sought by their bosses to get their views on policy.

Box 3   Alas, the world is full of idiots like this! They are very senior managers, and yet spend most of their time running around with buckets of water putting out fires.

   Such people only survive in growth conditions, because then they never actually have to *think deeply* about what they are doing. As soon as the going gets tough however, the 'headless chicken' syndrome sets in. They just rush around, faster and faster, until they eventually get found out as being the mental midgets they always were.

Box 4   People like this are generally real *directors*. They see their role in life as leaving the company in a healthier state than when they found it. They spend a lot of their time thinking about how the company can develop a *sustainable* competitive advantage. They are true strategists, at the same time as having an eye for detail.

Note

The above diagnosis is only really applicable to larger companies. In small companies, the levels of seniority are non-existent because there is only the boss, owner manager, proprietor or whatever title fits the bill. He or she is likely to spend time on strategic or tactical issues as and when the need arises. For such people to sit down quietly to address strategic issues is often something of a luxury, but they should strive to do so.

3   Strategic focus

The goal of all organizations, no matter in what terms it is dressed, is success. However, it can be shown that the time span over which success is to be achieved can vary from one company to another. While at first sight the time perspective might appear to make little difference, in practice it can have a profound effect on many aspects of business life. This matrix shows how the striving for success in the short, medium and long term can alter the company's strategic focus and even influence the corporate culture.

| Business activities | Focus for success | | |
	Short term	Medium term	Long term
Objectives	Short-term profit	Medium-term profit	Innovation
Management focus	Productivity	Beat competition	New product/markets
Target market	Existing customers	Competitor's customers	New customers
Energy directed at	Own staff	Competition	The unknown future
Differential advantage	Cost control	Segmentation	Differentiation
Key component of mix	Price	Promotion/place	Product
Organizational culture	Financial	Marketing	Entrepreneurial

4 · Product/market strategy – (the Ansoff matrix)

This matrix is one of those we termed a 'classic' in our introduction. What it provides is a framework which enables an organization to analyse its marketing objectives, since marketing objectives should be concerned only with what is sold, (the 'product'), and who it is sold to, (the 'market'). Where a marketing objective is positioned on this matrix not only provides implicit advice regarding the correct strategy which will need to be pursued, but it also gives some clues about how and where organizational strengths need to be developed.

```
                        Products
                   Existing      New

        Existing      1           2

Markets

        New           3           4
```

Box 1   A company developing a strategy around existing products and markets can grow its business by two means,

   improved productivity
   market penetration

Box 2   Here, a company, discovering that it cannot grow satisfactorily in box 1 can develop new products to introduce to its existing markets. Implicit in this strategy is that the company has the necessary capacity in terms of creativity, technical prowess and manufacturing.

Box 3   In order to obtain satisfactory growth, here, the company chooses to introduce its existing products or technology into new markets or applications. Implicit in this strategy is that the company possesses the necessary marketing expertise.

Box 4   Here the company has given up all hope of building on the known and introduces new products to new markets, ... a desperate move. History is littered with epitaphs to companies who failed to make diversification work.

Note

When using this matrix, as a rule of thumb, always exhaust all opportunities in box 1 before spending too much management time on the other boxes.

Box 2 is often an easier option than box 3, because it is *relationships with customers and markets* that make profits, *not* products.

Box 4 is generally something of an ego-trip for the chief executive, and is usually sold off or closed by his successor. The new chief executive, will, of course, in turn choose to make his or her own mistakes!

10

5 • The Boston matrix

The title of this matrix is derived from the Boston Consulting Group, who developed and used this approach with much success. It combines ideas which have profound implications for an organization, especially in terms of cash flow. It requires users to plot their products' market share (relative to the biggest market leader's share) along the horizontal axis. On the vertical axis, the rate of growth of the market in which each product competes should be plotted.

Relative market share

	High	Low
High	2	1
Low	3	4

Market growth

Box 1 Known by several names, such as *'problem child'*, *'question mark'*, *'wildcat'*, it could also be called the *'ulcer box!'* All new products and services should start here (market share will be low by definition, and it would be risky to aim for markets with low growth). Here you should selectively

- launch an attack on a narrow front *not* act like a leader, leadership is unimportant
- co-ordinate all your efforts
- keep it simple

Guerilla tactics are called for here.

Box 2 If they are successful, products or services from box 1 will eventually make it to box 2. They are now market leaders in a growing market.
This is popularly known as the *'star'* box, but could equally be called the *'glory'* box. Here you should

- develop the product or service
- invest in R&D
- extend credit (if necessary)
- keep competitors off balance
- promote aggressively

Above all, *aggression* is the watchword. There are no medals for going to sea with the biggest fleet and losing the battle!

11

Box 3   All good things eventually come to an end and the star product or service is no exception. In time, the market for it starts to fall, even though the product maintains its high market share.

   This box is generally called the 'cash cow', but it would be equally appropriate to call it the 'banker'. Continuing the sea battle analogy, you have seen off the opposing forces. Furthermore, the relatively low market growth is not a sufficient prize to attract new battle fleets out of port. In such circumstances, you should

- prune the product/service range
- segment and target more appropriately
- reduce costs (but not unreasonably)
- tighten credit
- reduce accounts receivable
- increase inventory turnover

Don't milk products or services in this box, but *do* defend and maintain. Have a mobile defence force.

Box 4   Popularly called the 'dog' box, althought 'lost cause' would be equally descriptive. Any investment into products or services in this box is likely to be a case of throwing good money after bad.

   Tactical surprise is your only hope, especially where your larger competitors are so complacent as to appear asleep.

Note

This 'snapshot' of a company's product (or service) portfolio shows how its products are distributed on this matrix. The significance of doing this is that only those products in the *cash cow* box will be net generators of funds. All other boxes will be in cash-flow deficit, or at best, neutral.

The Boston matrix can also be used to forecast the market position of products in, say, five years from now, if current policies are followed. The following diagram illustrates how this is achieved.

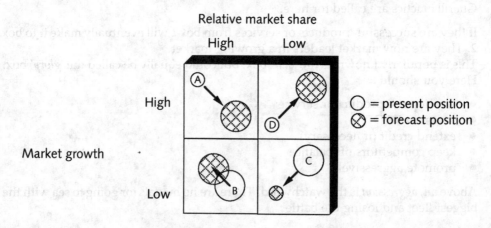

Relative market share

High   Low

High

Market growth

Low

○ = present position
⊗ = forecast position

The area of each circle is proportional to each product's contribution to the total sales volume. In the above example, the company is following what could prove to be disastrous policies in respect to its product portfolio management.

Products A and D although growing, are losing market share in what are still high-growth markets. Products B and C are gaining market share in declining markets.

To accept a lower than market growth rate for product A clearly demonstrates that the company is failing to be competitive enough, perhaps because it is putting too many resources in to trying to make product D a success, something it is failing to achieve.

Likewise, to push for market share in low-growth markets (products B and C) will lead to unnecessary price wars and market disruption.

6 · The directional policy matrix

However useful the previous Boston matrix has proved to be, many companies find it extremely difficult to use it effectively. This is because market share and market growth are not always easy to measure with any degree of accuracy.

The directional policy matrix helps to overcome this problem. It achieves similar results to the Boston matrix, but uses slightly different parameters.

Business strengths have to be considered in relative terms when compared to your main competitors. Market attractiveness can be measured in terms of any criteria that make sense for the future profitability and/or health of your particular business.

Business strengths

		High	Low
	High	2	3
Market attractiveness	Low	1	4

Box 1 Here you have high strengths in a market which has lost its attractiveness, in terms of future potential. However, it's a good box for any part of your business to be in, so maintain your position here for as long as you can.

Box 2 Obviously the best box of all. Here your strengths are directed at highly attractive markets. Invest your best resources in those parts of your business which are in this box.

Box 3 This is an uncomfortable place to be. You find the market potential attractive, but do not have the business strengths that are necessary for being really successful. The options facing you are either,

- take what you can, while you can, or
- invest in building a better competitive position

You will probably have to be selective, as it will cost you to invest in every aspect of your business.

Box 4 Think carefully about what you are doing to be in this box at all. Low in market potential, and where you have few strengths. Only keep those parts of your business which are in this box if they are supporting more profitable parts (for example, if they complete a product range). Another reason for keeping them might be if they are absorbing overhead costs.

Note

How market attractiveness and business strengths are measured will clearly be related to the circumstances of each individual organization. However, here are some of the possible factors which will need to be considered.

Market attractiveness

Market factors

Size, growth rate, price sensitivity, seasonality, cyclicality, bargaining power of buyers and/or distributors, etc.

Competition

Type, number, ease of entry, substitute products, likelihood of new technology, market share/domination, etc.

Financial and Economic

Margins, possible economies of scale, capacity utilization, financial barriers to entry etc.

Technological

Patents and copyrights, required technology, complexity, maturity, volatility, etc.

Socio-political

Social attitudes and trends, laws and regulations. Influence of pressure groups, human factors, etc.

Business strengths

These will be how, when compared to its main competitors, the company rates against the critical success factors (i.e. the key things that any company competing for business *must* get right in order to succeed); such factors might include image; reputation; design capability; product reliability; quality standards; service levels; ability to respond to new demands; facilities; location; pricing policy; product range and so on.

Both market attractiveness and business strengths can be quantified by scoring and weighting the selected criteria. Here are examples of how this can be done.

Market attractiveness evaluation

Key factors	Scoring criteria*	Raw score	Weighting (%)*	Weighted score
Market size (£M)	≤ £50 <———> ≥ £250	5	30	1.5
Competitive intensity	High <———> Low	7	20	1.4
Industry profitability	≤ 10% <———> ≥ 15%	8	40	3.2
Cyclicality	High <———> Low	3	10	0.3
			Total	6.4

Notes

* Scoring criteria covers a range of 10 points between two limits shown, i.e. for market size ≤ £50 = 0 and ≥ £250 = 10.

** The total weighting has to equal 100 per cent. In this example, industry profitability is seen to be the most important factor and carries a 40 per cent weighting. In comparison, competitive intensity is seen as only half as important, and carries a weighting of 20 per cent.

The total market attractiveness score in this example, 6.4, would place this market in the highly attractive category, since 5.0 would be the mid-point.

Business strengths evaluation

Critical success factors	Weighting (%)	Our company		Company A		Company B	
Product	20	9	1.8	6	1.2	4	0.8
Price	10	8	0.8	5	0.5	10	1.0
Service	50	5	2.5	9	4.5	6	3.0
Image	20	8	1.6	8	1.6	3	0.6
		Total	6.7		7.8		5.4

Note

Again the scoring is on a 10 point scale. Thus, in this example, our company scores high (9 points) on product, but with a weighting of 20 per cent, the weighted score becomes 1.8.

The totals reveal that competitor A is stronger than us, whereas competitor B is weaker.

However, because we are interested in relative business strengths in this instance it is meaningless to accept 5.0 as the mid-point. Instead, the mid-line is drawn at a point which is the average for the leading players in the market. In this example that would be $(6.7 + 7.8 + 5.4):3 = 6.66$.

On this basis, our company is just about average in terms of relative business strengths. Equally, we can see that service has to be considerably improved if we are to compete effectively.

7 · Business risk analysis

The lesson to be learned from the Ansoff matrix is that the riskiest option of all is to strive for new products into new markets (i.e. diversification). A proverb can be quoted to back this argument 'the cobbler should stick to his last', but more recently it has become fashionable in management circles to talk about getting back to the 'core business'.

The core business is therefore centred around manufacturing know-how and expertise, design capability, technology, skills of the workforce, and so on.

By implication, the successful current products must be the benchmark for the core business. Any new products can thus be assessed in terms of how close or distant they come in terms of compatibility with the core business. So, for example, a new product which required investment in a new technology, and whose design was beyond the scope of the current design department, could be described as remote from the core business.

This idea of closeness to the core business and the concept of market attractiveness, from the directional policy matrix, can be usefully combined to analyse the risk of investing in new products.

Closeness to core business

	Close	Distant
High	1	2
Low	3	4

Market attractiveness

Before using the matrix, criteria have to be established regarding what constitutes the parameters of the core business. For example, technology, familiarity with the materials, special finishes, quality standards, and so on.

Market attractiveness criteria will probably be concerned with factors like size, prospects for growth, ease of entry, level of competition, and the like.

Potential new products are then considered against these two sets of criteria and are plotted on the matrix.

Box 1 Products which fall into this category fall very much in line with the core business criteria and have a high market attractiveness potential. These will be ideal products to develop and represent the least risk.

Box 2 Products falling into this box are distant from the core business, even though they are high in the market attractiveness scale. Clearly, such products are going to be

17

risky to develop and will need a high level of investment, both in terms of resources and expertise. The only justification for proceeding is if the long-term corporate strategy is to develop in this way.

Box 3   Products here are close to the core business, but low on market attractiveness. These products are not risky in terms of manufacturing, but whether or not to proceed will be based on a commercial evaluation of the market potential.

       The low market attractiveness is not necessarily a bad thing, since it will make it less promising ground for competitors.

Box 4   Products in this box represent poor prospects, in whatever way they are viewed. They depart from the core business and offer low market attractiveness.

8 Competitive advantage (Porter) ·

This matrix looks at how an organization might gain a competitive advantage on the basis of its relative costs, and/or the degree to which it can differentiate its products/services from those of its competitors.

Relative costs

		High	Low
Degree of differentiation of product/service	**High**	3	2
	Low	4	1

Box 1   What you are selling is much like your competitor's products or services. However, you have the advantage of being the lowest cost producer and, while you can sustain that 'edge', you can be successful.

Box 2   This is the 'outstanding success' box. You enjoy both low costs and high differentiation.

Box 3   This is for the specialist who cannot possibly be a low cost producer, but who can offer products or services with significant differences from those of competitors.

Box 4   This is of course, the *'idiot box'*. High costs and a commodity type of product are the ingredients for disaster. Organizations here might survive if they happen to be in growth markets.

Note

Box 1 producers, unless they are offering a lower price, *must* by definition also have some differences, so beware. Box 3 producers must *also* be cost effective if they are to survive. It is important to remember that there are niche markets, not niche companies.

9   Competitive strategy

This matrix builds on matrix 8 and considers how marketing strategy can be influenced by the relationship between the nature of a company's competitive advantage, and the diversity of its market.

Basis of
competitive advantage

		Differ-entiation	Costs
Number of market segments	Many	1	2
	Few	3	4

Box 1   Here the strategy will have to be to continue to seek a differential advantage over competing offers. Thus, there should be an emphasis on getting close to customers and understanding their requirements and/or building in added benefits.

Box 2   Here the strategy needs to be to win overall cost leadership. This requires the company to be slicker and fitter than its competitors.

Box 3   Here a strategy similar to box 1 will be required. The difference here is that the company pursues a strategy of focus.

Box 4   The strategy required in this box will be to focus on costs and not to let any current advantage slip away. The company seeks to gain cost advantage by focusing on a few segments.

10 Market forces

From time to time, there is a need for companies to review their markets. By positioning each market on this matrix, it becomes possible to assess its longer term viability, and subsequent value to the company.

Probability of new entrants/substitutes

	High	Low
High	4	3
Low	1	2

Power of buyers

Box 1 Here the probability of these kinds of markets attracting new entrants or substitute products/services is high, probably because the power of the buyers is low. One reason for this could be that you have made an attractive (to the customer) techno-logical breakthrough which competitors will be quick to emulate. In this case, either make your profit now while the going is good, or go for market share so you can enjoy low costs and hence be in a better position to fight off the challenges of new entrants.

Box 2 This is the very best kind of market (from a manufacturer's point of view), as not only is the power of buyers low, but there is little likelihood of new entrants or substitute products/services for some time. The reason is probably that you have a technological lead or dominant market position. Clearly, you should strive for such market positions as they are likely to be extremely profitable.

Box 3 Here, the power of buyers is high, which may well explain why the likelihood of new entrants is low. This is probably because the market is mature or that there is too much production/supply capacity, leading to declining prices and profit margins. It would also explain why buyers are so powerful. The best strategy is to aim to differentiate your products/services in some way at the same time as creating demand pull through promotion, so as to gain more power over buyers.

Box 4 This is the worst possible market situation of all, with buyers having high power and new entrants/substitutes coming along in a continuous stream, so making the situation even worse. But you need to consider why they are coming into such an unattractive market (in profit margin/terms). Is it because the market is destined to grow dramatically? If so, your best strategy may well be to grin and bear the low profits and go for market share leadership, which should lead to corresponding low costs. Eventually, you should reap your reward, as smaller competitors drop out, so giving you more power over buyers!

11 Objectives priority

The limit on resources is always a barrier to what companies can and cannot achieve. However, because resources always have to be 'rationed', this matrix provides some guidance about how this might be done.

		Urgency of objectives		
		Low	Medium	High
	Minor	9	8	6
Impact of objectives	Significant	7	5	3
	Major	4	2	1

Possible time/resource allocation (%)

The boxes are numbered 1 to 9. Having set your objectives, you should think very carefully about how you should position each one on the above matrix. Having done this, we suggest that you consider allocating time and resources to each box along the following lines.

Box 1	30%	Box 4	12%	Box 7	8%
Box 2	15%	Box 5	10%	Box 8	4%
Box 3	12%	Box 6	8%	Box 9	1%
	57%		30%		13%

By doing this, time and resources will be absorbed in a way that is roughly proportional to the importance of each objective.

12 Strategic issues priority

Using similar reasoning to the previous matrix, a company cannot hope to respond equally well to all the strategic issues which face it. As in most other aspects of its business, priorities have to be established. This matrix provides a framework for setting such priorities.

Impact of strategic issues

		Low	Significant	Major
	Low	1	2	3
Urgency of strategic issues	Significant	4	5	6
	Pressing	7	8	9

First make a list (which can be as long as you like) of the issues which you or your organization face. Next, assign them to one of the nine boxes based on your assessment of their impact (low, significant, or major), and on their degree of urgency (low, significant, or pressing).

Box 1 Drop from your list – are you *sure* you've got it right?

Box 2 Just carry out a periodic review.

Box 3 Monitor these continuously.

Box 4 Drop these, or carry out a periodic review.

Box 5 Carry out a periodic review or monitor.

Box 6 Plan a delayed response.

Box 7 Monitor.

Box 8 Monitor continuously.

Box 9 Respond *immediately*.

23

13 Opportunities matrix

The next two matrices should be read in conjunction with matrix 15.

The marketer has to look into the future and try to make sense of what can be seen. Both opportunities and threats are of particular interest, because it is they which influence future success and/or failure.

The perfect 'crystal ball' has yet to be invented. Nevertheless, these two matrices will help you to resolve an uncertain future in a more quantifiable form.

Impact on the organization

	10	1
0.9	4	3
0.1	1	2

Probability of occurrence

Step 1   Make a comprehensive list of all possible issues/events which could provide your organization with an opportunity for creating some kind of competitive advantage. It could, for example, be declining raw material prices or a change in government legislation. The list is limitless.

Step 2   Allocate a number between 1 and 10 to each opportunity, with 10 representing the most favourable impact on the organization and 1 hardly any favourable impact.

Step 3   Now allocate a number between 0.1 and 0.9 to each opportunity to indicate your considered view about the probability of their occurrence during the next three years. Some are obviously much more likely to occur than others. This different scale is required because we are considering probabilities. A zero score would indicate that the opportunity will never occur. Similarly a 1.0 score would mean that it was a certainty.

Step 4   Plot each opportunity you have listed on the above matrix. Use a code letter to designate each opportunity.

Box 1   Should any of these opportunities occur, make sure you have a plan. However, as they are unlikely to occur during the next three years, just keep a watching brief.

Box 2   Don't be too concerned about these opportunities, as not only are they not likely to happen, but even if they do, their impact on your organization isn't very great. Ignore these.

Box 3   These opportunities will probably occur during the next three years, but will not have a great impact on the organization. Nonetheless, as they *are* opportunities, and as they are likely to occur, make sure you're ready to take full advantage of them when they do.

Box 4   The best box of all, as not only are these opportunities likely to occur, but they will have a big impact on your organization. In which case, you'd better be prepared for them. Here, it is suggested that you prepare a number of action plans setting out exactly who will do what and when. Then press the '*go*' button when the opportunity occurs.

14   Threats matrix

Impact on the organization

	10	1
0.9	4	3
0.1	1	2

Probability of
occurrence

Step 1 Make a comprehensive list of all possible issues/events which could provide your organization with a threat for creating some kind of competitive disadvantage. It could, for example, be increasing raw material prices or a change in government legislation. The list is limitless.

Step 2 Allocate a number between 0.1 and 0.9 to each threat with 10 representing the most unfavourable impact on the organization and 1 hardly any impact.

Step 3 Now allocate a number between 1 and 10 to each threat to indicate your considered view about the probability of their occurrence during the next three years. Some are obviously much more likely to occur than others. This different scale is required because we are considering probabilities. A zero score would indicate that the opportunity will never occur. Similarly a 1.0 score would mean that it was a certainty.

Step 4 Plot each threat you have listed on the above matrix. Use a code letter to designate each threat.

Box 1 Should any of these threats occur, make sure you have a plan. However, as they are unlikely to occur during the next three years, just keep a watching brief.

Box 2 Don't be too concerned about these threats, as not only are they not likely to happen, but even if they do, their impact on your organization isn't very great. Ignore these.

Box 3 These threats will probably occur during the next three years, but will not have a great impact on the organization. Nonetheless, as they *are* threats, and as they are likely to occur, make sure you're ready to respond to them when they do.

Box 4 The worst box of all, as not only are these threats likely to occur, but they will have a big impact on your organization. In which case, you'd better be prepared for them. Here, it is suggested that you prepare a number of action plans setting out exactly who will do what and when. Then press the '*go*' button when the threat occurs.

15 Gap analysis (revenue)

The purpose of this matrix is to help you to plan for growth. You will observe that the axes aren't labelled here because, as you will see, it is an amended and quantified version of the Ansoff matrix. This first gap analysis matrix is for *revenue*. The next is for *profit*.

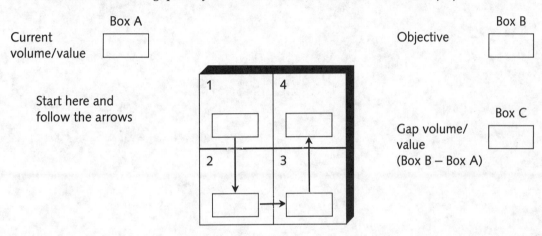

To use the matrix, start by putting in box A a figure which represents your current output in either volume or value terms. Next put a figure in box B (either volume or value) which represents your objective in three years' time. It is essential that you should be ambitious in setting your objective and that you should make it as challenging as possible. Now subtract A from B and put the resulting sum in box C. This is the size of the gap to be filled. You are now ready to use the matrix to close this gap.

Box 1 Box 1 is concerned with existing products and existing markets. There are two actions you can take, you can improve productivity, and/or you can improve your market share. To work out how much additional revenue you can get from productivity, estimate how much business you could get from a better product mix, a better customer mix, increasing prices, improving the call rate and effectiveness of your sales force, charging for delivery and so on. Next estimate how much additional business you could get from better market penetration. It is often better if this is done on a product-by-product/customer-by-customer basis. If the addition of productivity and market penetration does not fill the gap (box C), continue down to box 2.

Box 2 For box 2, estimate the additional business you could get from new products for your existing markets, then do the same for existing products for new markets. If the addition of both of these seems (plus box 1 above) still does not fill the gap (box C), continue across to box 3.

Box 3 Estimate the additional business you could get from a combination of new products for new markets (diversification). If this still does not fill the gap (box C), continue up to box 4.

Box 4   Box 4 represents the last chance you've got for filling the gap. Here, you will need to consider investing in new assets to fill the gap. This could be acquisition, licensing, or a joint venture of some kind. You should by now have filled the gap. If you haven't, consider whether you have been sufficiently rigorous in doing the exercise. If you have, then consider reducing the objective! Alternatively perhaps you should consider getting out of this business altogether.

16 Gap analysis (profit)

This second gap analysis matrix focuses on profit, but is tackled in the same way as the preceding matrix.

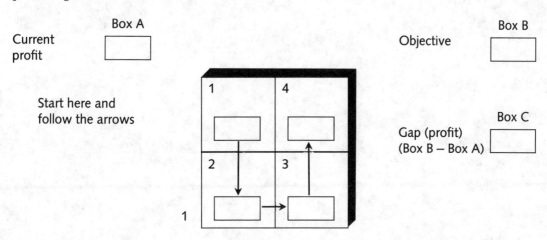

Current profit — Box A

Objective — Box B

Start here and follow the arrows

Gap (profit) (Box B − Box A) — Box C

Box 1 For box 1, since again it is concerned with existing products and markets there are two actions you can take, you can improve productivity, and/or you can improve your market share. To work out how much additional profit you can get from productivity. Next estimate how much additional profit you could get from better market penetration. It is often better if this is done on a product-by-product/customer-by-customer basis. If the addition of productivity and market penetration does not fill the gap (box C), continue down to box 2.

Box 2 For box 2, estimate the additional business profit you could get from new products for your existing markets, then do the same for existing products for new markets. If the addition of both of these seems (plus box 1 above) still does not fill the gap (box C), continue across to box 3.

Box 3 Estimate the additional business you could get from a combination of new products for new markets (diversification). If this still does not fill the gap (box C), continue up to box 4.

Box 4 Box 4 represents the last chance you've got for filling the gap. Here, you will need to consider investing in new assets to fill the gap. This could be acquisition or a joint venture of some kind. You should by now have filled the gap. If you haven't, consider whether you have been sufficiently vigorous in doing the exercise. If you have, then consider reducing the objective! Alternatively, perhaps you should consider getting out of this business altogether.

2 Organizational issues

17 Organizational culture

It can be shown that organizations follow a life cycle in the same way as products. As they go through the different stages of development, growth, maturity and decline, it is possible to detect changes in the 'culture', or the way the organization responds to situations. This matrix can be useful in establishing where the organization might be in terms of its life cycle. Knowing this enables management to start an organizational renewal programme, if it is appropriate to do so.

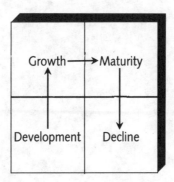

Development Here the company is small and informal, very flexible in the way it responds to situations. Creativity is the mother of invention, driven by a necessity through lack of resources. Few systems and procedures. The CEO is close to customers and everything else which takes place. The overall direction might lurch from time to time as the company responds to the demands of its largest customers. If the original idea behind the company is a good one, it can be a very profitable enterprise.

Growth Here this is a clear sense of purpose and direction, coupled with a drive for efficiency. There is a high level of motivation, which gives rise to a productive organization. Management is shrewd and professional. Profits are ploughed back and growth rate can be dramatic. Market segmentation is introduced to make the aggressive sales effort more effective.

Maturity Here complacency begins to seep into organizational life. Investment in the company falls, especially in new products and R&D. Cash is frittered away on high wages and peripheral items. '*Stars*' are treated as '*cash cows*'. Market dominance as a policy is abandoned and the status quo is accepted. Overheads increase and there is general mismanagement and inefficiency. Ground is given to competitors through inadequate service and deteriorating quality of goods.

Decline Because of mismanagement, old plant, etc., costs have risen. Unit costs have increased because of falling sales volume. Customers begin to lose faith in the company, whose co-ordination and control seems to break down frequently. Investment in R&D is non-existent. There is a perennial cash flow crisis, and management is by panic measures. The company has to operate with increasingly lower margins because of its costs and non-competitive position.

18 Marketing effectiveness

This matrix is designed to help you to make the best decisions about ways to improve your marketing effectiveness. It is adapted from a technique known as force-field analysis which was developed by Kurt Lewin.

Driving forces

	Low	High
Restraining forces High	1	2
Restraining forces Low	3	4

Definitions

Driving forces are all those factors that are 'pushing' for, or encouraging, an improvement in your marketing effectiveness.

Examples of driving forces might be a motivation to improve, or a strong desire to stay competitive, or top management backing for marketing initiatives, a large pool of creative talent in the organization, and so on.

Restraining forces are those factors which militate against improvements in your marketing effectiveness. They are barriers to improvement.

Examples of restraining forces might be lack of marketing skills, uncompetitive products, over-concentration on financial aspects of the business and so on.

This matrix provides a conceptual framework and does not require you to plot anything.

Box 1 Here you have high restraining forces and low driving forces. Your strategy for improvement must be to reduce the restraining forces and to increase the driving forces in *just one or two areas* where they will make a high impact.

Box 2 Here you already have high driving forces and so your strategy has to be to give them an opportunity to work. Therefore concentrate entirely on reducing restraining forces.

Box 3 There really is no momentum for change here. If you wanted to bring about change, then you would have to invigorate the driving forces.

Box 4 The driving forces are naturally going to win through. This is a healthy position to be in.

19 Marketing politics

Introducing marketing planning or changes of strategy can be a stab to the very centre of the organization. The marketer needs to be aware of how, what to him, are seemingly obvious ideas, are going to make impact on the organization as a whole. Moreover, it is worth knowing on which issues to fight and where to be more circumspect.

Acceptability to organization

	Low	High
High	1	2
Low	4	3

Importance to marketer

Box 1 Here the proposed action is of high importance to the marketer, but has a low level of acceptance to the organization. It is the biggest area of conflict. There are two broad options:

- re-evaluate the proposal; is it just a bee in the marketer's bonnet or is it really important?

- sell hard to gain acceptance. This will mean establishing who constitutes the decision making unit (DMU) and selling the proposition to each member in terms of the benefits they value.

There will be a need to produce much factual evidence, because opinions will not carry any weight.

Box 2 There should be no problems here. The marketer will probably be praised for his perception at realizing what was required.

Box 3 Here the acceptability to the organization is high, but the issue is relatively unimportant to the marketer. Items that fall into this category can earn the marketer much credibility, and as long as they don't detract from really important issues the marketer should pursue them. Success in this box might help his case in box 1.

Box 4 This is the 'why bother' box. It is not worth pursuing anything which falls into this area.

20 The climate for marketing planning

The 'climate' in which marketing planning operates can be coloured by many factors. Not least among these are the results the company has been achieving, and the decision maker's belief or expectations about what marketing planning might achieve.

This matrix explores how these two factors can combine.

Previous results

	Poor	Good
High	1	2
Low	3	4

People's beliefs/
expectations of
marketing planning

Box 1 The *'frustration'* box. The poor results are an extreme disappointment for those who expect so much from marketing planning. There are two options facing companies in this box:

- re-examine the marketing planning process and levels of skill of those involved . . . and take corrective action.
- give the planning process more time to deliver the goods (we have found that it can take up to three years for a company to introduce marketing planning successfully).

Box 2 The *'smug'* box, or *'aren't we great'*. The company is getting the results from marketing planning which were expected. The danger facing it is that complacency might set in.

Box 3 The *'self-fulfilling prophecy'* box, or *'I told you it would never work'*. It is difficult to see how a company can be rescued from this position without resorting to the corporate equivalent of brain surgery.

Box 4 A strange combination of forces at work here. It might be indicative of a company in transition from box 3. Alternatively it might be that the company, by happy co-incidence, happens to be in the right place at the right time, i.e. it has a product or service for which there is a great demand.

21 Formality of the marketing plan

A marketing plan is at the heart of successful marketing. However, the degree of formality of such a plan is very much dependent on the company situation and its culture. This matrix provides some guidance on just how formal a marketing plan needs to be.

		Company size	
		Small	Large
	High	1	2
Complexity of products/ markets			
	Low	3	4

Box 1 Although any form of systematic planning is rarely found in small companies, the high complexity of products/markets implies that some form of plan is required here. However, in such a small company, this doesn't have to be a massive bureaucratic process.

Box 2 Here, the case is different. In large companies, it is essential for everyone to know who does 'what' and 'when'. The problems of co-ordinating resources and communicating requirements in complex situations, need to be embraced in a formalized planning system.

Box 3 Here it could be argued that, should it exist, a marketing plan would be of minimal formality. Perhaps a simple sales plan would be the only useful requirement.

Box 4 The formality of a marketing plan in this box is less critical than for box 2. However, some form of plan will probably benefit communications among staff. The inclination towards formal planning will in all likelihood be a reflection of the corporate culture, rather than a situational necessity.

Note

It is possible, that a company can be dealing with some products/markets which are highly complex and some which are relatively simple. The implication is that it doesn't need a 'sledgehammer' marketing plan for cracking the simple 'nut' market. The message is, don't over-complicate the planning process where it doesn't need it.

22 Modes of marketing planning matrix

There are many different approaches to marketing planning. This matrix explores the relationship between an organization's concern for the plan, and the extent to which it is concerned to involve its staff.

```
                        Concern for
                     marketing planning

                      Low        High

              High      1          2

Concern for
involving staff

              Low       3          4
```

Box 1   Here there is a low corporate concern for planning, but a climate for involving staff. This is a recipe for *anarchy*. Without some form of corporate guidance, the high quality and motivated contributions from below could pull the company in many different directions.

Box 2   This is an *ideal* combination which is found in most companies where marketing planning is used with success. Here the company is making best use of up-to-date information available to its staff, but within the framework of a planning process which is given high visibility.

Box 3   The *'apathy'* box. Clearly the investment in marketing planning is minimal and is likely to be a complete waste of time.

Box 4   This can be a very *bureaucratic* approach to marketing planning, where the concern for the planning process transcends all else. This 'top down' approach can easily deteriorate into the annual 'numbers game', unless the hearts and minds of staff are won over. An alternative which fits into this box is the 'ivory tower' mode of planning. Here a senior executive labours long and hard behind closed doors, only to emerge weeks later with a plan which can be fatally flawed because of inaccurate, or out-of-date, input information.

23 Types of marketing department

Marketing departments do not always perform the same role in their organizations. We have found that, to a large extent, what a department does is prescribed by its size, and the degree of responsibility it has. It is these issues which are explored in this matrix.

Consider in which box you would place your marketing department. Then compare the role you expect of it with the comments in that box. In the light of this information, is there a suggestion that you expect too much or too little from your marketing department?

Size of marketing department

	Small	Large
High	1	2
Low	3	4

Responsibilities

Box 1 Here you have a small department, with a high level of responsibility. This suggests that it ought to be involved in providing services associated with strategic issues.

Box 2 Departments in this box have a high level of responsibility and enough staff to offer an integrated, full-service marketing input.

Box 3 The limited nature of departments in this box, both in terms of responsibility and size, will dictate that their organizational input will be reduced. They will be likely to do little other than to offer a modest support function.

Box 4 The relatively low level of responsibility, coupled with large size, suggests that marketing departments in this box will be heavily involved in selling-orientated support marketing.

24 Sources of marketing information

Information is the 'life blood' of effective decision making. While managers often complain that they are starved of information, this is rarely the case. There is usually an abundance of information, but it is not in the right format to be readily digestible.

This matrix shows the origins and the nature of information that can be made available.

Origin of information

	Internal	External
Historical	1	2
Original	3	4

Nature of information

Box 1   Internal information of an historical nature can be obtained from sales records, customer analysis sheets, sales representative's reports, complaints, and so on.

Box 2   A prime source of external historical data are government statistics, but equally there are journals, directories and databases which can be used. Trade associations and chambers of commerce can also be useful sources of this type of information.

Box 3   Internal information of an original nature would be the results of experimentation, for example, with parts of the marketing mix, specific market research, or test marketing.

Box 4   Original external information would be that provided by industry experts or specific customer or market surveys, commissioned by trade associations or their equivalents.

25 Choosing a market research organization

Market research is a specialized activity and, for this reason, many organizations use outside agencies when they need it. This matrix provides some ideas about the issues to be considered when seeking a market research organization.

Quality of staff and resources

	1	10
10	1	2
1	3	4

Experience
and reputation

Instructions

Step 1 Make a list of the market research organizations from which you will be selecting.

Step 2 Consider the factors about experience and reputation which could influence your choice. These might include:

- reputation of the firm in general
- reputation in your industry
- what their clients tell you
- their standing among professional bodies
- number of their clients in your type of business
- how long established
- published articles
- association with new developments
- association with prestigious clients/academic institutions
- amount of repeat business . . . and so on

Step 3 List which of these factors are the most significant for you. Give these factors a weighting (as a percentage) showing their relative importance.

Step 4 Score each potential MR organization between 1 and 10 (most favourable) against these factors. Multiply each factor score by its weighting factor.

Step 5 Add up the total weighted scores for each organization. You can plot these on the vertical scale of the matrix.

Step 6   Consider factors about quality of staff and resources which could affect your choice. Such factors could include:

- financial standing
- number of full-time staff
- qualifications of staff
- total size of interview force
- location of premises
- condition of premises
- equipment available
- involvement of senior staff on projects
- regional network . . . and so on

Step 7   Apply the same thinking and calculations to these factors as steps 3, 4 and 5 did for experience and reputation.

Step 8   Plot the total weighted scores for each MR organization along the horizontal axis.

Step 9   Plot each organization on the matrix, using the vertical and horizontal axis scores to establish the exact position.

Box 1   MR organizations in this box have satisfied you about their experience but not the quality of their staff. It would be better to renew your search.

Box 2   Organizations in this box would seem to be ideally suited to your requirements.

Box 3   Do not touch these organizations, even with the proverbial 'barge pole'.

Box 4   These organizations satisfy your quality criteria, but not on experience and reputation. This being the case, it would be better to continue your search.

3 Products and services

26 Product differentiation/cost

If the company pursues a strategy of product/service differentiation, it is likely to incur some degree of additional cost. It is also likely that not every attempt to differentiate the product/service will be equally valued by customers. This matrix explores the range of possibilities which exist.

Cost to company to provide

	High	Low
High	3	2
Low	4	1

Perceived value by customer

Instructions

In order to complete this matrix it is necessary to comply with the following.

Step 1 List the features of your products or services and what you consider to be their advantages over those of your competitors.

Step 2 Get your accountant to give you an indication of the real *cost* of providing these differences.

Step 3 Check with your customers how highly they value these differences.

Step 4 Plot each of the features in the appropriate cost/value box.

Box 1 This isn't too bad, because although these differences are not very highly valued by your customers, they don't cost a lot to provide. A break-even situation?

Box 2 This is obviously the best box of all, as these highly valued differences don't cost you much to provide. Well done, this is first-class marketing.

Box 3 Beware! Although these differences are highly valued by customers, they also cost a lot to provide. Look carefully at your costs.

Box 4 What on earth are you doing this for? It's costing you an arm and a leg and the customer doesn't care anyway!

27 Improving non-differentiated products/services

Several other matrices have referred to the difficulty of being competitive with 'me-too' products or services. For those that want to improve their situation, there are two broad options open to them. This matrix explores what a move to differentiation can mean in practical terms. This matrix is more a conceptual framework than something on which you have to position your product.

Ease of differentiating product

	Difficult	Possible
Possible	1	2
Difficult	3	4

Ease of differentiating marketing

Box 1 Here you are stuck with the product, but see a possibility of differentiating it by the way it is marketed. In effect, you will be attempting not to sell a sausage, but its sizzle. The notes below might provide you with some ideas.

Box 2 Here you can see distinct possibilities for differentiating the product or services as well as the way it is marketed and things shouldn't be too much of a problem.

Box 3 Here, you are really stuck. You are in something like the 'commodity trap'. Your best strategy will be to seek cost reductions wherever you can and attempt to win cost leadership.

Box 4 Here, following the analogy in box 1, you can see ways to produce a 'better sausage'. Differentiating the product will be an easier task than seeking to change the way it is marketed. Again, the notes below may be a source of ideas.

Note

Here are some suggestions about ways in which a product or service might be differentiated, either directly, or through its marketing.

Ways to differentiate products/services

- improve the design
- provide more features

48

- provide more benefits/applications
- change colour
- change material
- make it easier to use
- improve quality
- improve durability
- provide add-ons/accessories
- extend range
- provide an element of service e.g. training, maintenance etc.

Ways to differentiate through marketing

- change price
- provide discounts
- offer/extend guarantee
- improve packaging
- change distribution channels
- improve service levels
- change advertising
- devise promotions
- change image of product/service

28 Life cycle – costs and market conditions

Market circumstances change over the life of a product, and so it follows that a company's strategies should also change accordingly. This matrix provides a set of 'snapshots' which describe cost and market conditions in relation to the life cycle phases.

Pricing, distribution and promotion all need to be reviewed against this matrix. For example, at the introduction phase, promotional efforts might need to concentrate on creating awareness for the product or service. Later in life, when awareness levels are high, it is likely that more effort will be required to position the product or service, by creating a particular image which differentiates it from the competition.

	Introduction	Growth	Maturity/ saturation	Decline
Costs	Can be high, due to inexperience in supplying and the cost of promotion.	Increasing due to increased volume and fighting off competition. High growth requires funding.	Stabilizing/ reducing as experience and reduced competition take effect.	Can be high if not managed due to diseconomies of scale e.g. only small runs.
Demand	Unpredictable. Forecasts can vary widely.	Upper limits might be forecast but volatile situation sensitive to prices and competition.	Fairly well defined.	Known and limited.
Competition	Largely unknown.	Many new entrants jump on 'bandwagon'. Competition fierce.	Marginal competitors leave. Remainder tend to specialize with particular segments.	New entrants are unlikely. Competition declines.
Customer loyalty	Trial usage, new relationship, little loyalty.	Some loyalty but to ensure supplies many customers might have more than one supplier.	Well-established buying patterns with high customer loyalty.	Extremely stable. Customers are not motivated to seek new suppliers.
Ease of entry	Relatively easy because market leaders have not yet emerged. Customers feeling their way.	More difficult as some suppliers begin to establish market share and benefit from economies of scale.	Difficult because of established buying patterns. New business has to be won.	Little incentive to enter.

29 New product/service launch (1)

This matrix is designed to guide those who are about to launch a new product or service. If the product is especially different from what is already well known, you should find this will save you a lot of time, money and wasted effort. You will have to use your experience about customers, or customer groups, to determine where you place them on this matrix.

Tendency to purchase

	High	Low
Favourable	4	3
Unfavourable	1	2

Attitude towards 'new' things

Box 1 By definition, anyone who falls in this box clearly needs their head examining! It is highly unlikely that many people will in fact want to buy.

Box 2 This box, on the other hand, is inhabited by most people in the early days of a new product launch (approximately 50 per cent). Clearly, it will be a waste of time spending too heavily on advertising and selling, as this group will not buy until such time as the product is in wide circulation and is reasonably priced.

Box 3 There are usually about 34 per cent of any population who are easily swayed by those whose opinions they admire. They are a crucial part of any market for new product introductions. Nonetheless, it is important to realize that there is an even more important section of the market (box 4).

Box 4 These people (about 16 per cent of the population) are the key to any new product launch. They consist of people that others look up to and admire. They tend to be better off, more innovative and open minded. They are always prepared to try new things and ideas, to which they give social approbation. Find out who these people are and concentrate all your efforts on this group.

Note

The percentage figures quoted above are abstracted from research conducted by Everett Rogers and form the basis of his theory about innovation diffusion.

30   New product/service launch (2)

As with many aspects of marketing, a balance has to be struck between what is in the proposal for the company, and what is in it for the customer. This matrix looks at return on investment and cost benefits to the customer.

Return on investment

	Negative	Positive
High	3	2
Low	4	1

Cost benefit to customer

Box 1   A high return on investment for the company launching the product, but a low cost/benefit for the customer. This is the *'buyer beware'* box. What on earth are people buying this for? It is unlikely to last for long as customers realize they are being duped.

Box 2   This is the best box of all, and the one we should all aim for. Here the company has a high return and the customer has a high benefit. Products launched into this box stand a high chance of success.

Box 3   This is the *'give away'* box (for the company), as the customer gets all the benefits and there's a negative return for the company. It is difficult to understand such a policy. The customer will go on buying the product just as long as the company is stupid enough to go on providing it (probably until it goes bankrupt!)

Box 4   This box has to be a *'fool's paradise'*, as not only is the company making a loss, but the customer is better off without it as well!

31 Brands, own label, generic products

Here, we look at the irksome problem of branded products versus own-label, versus generics. By using a little imagination, the issues involved can be represented in a matrix form. This particular matrix considers consumer's brand awareness and the perceived risk they attach to the buying decision. Against this framework, three boxes, which approximately represent generic products (box 1), own-label products (box 2) and brand leaders (box 3), can be hypothesized.

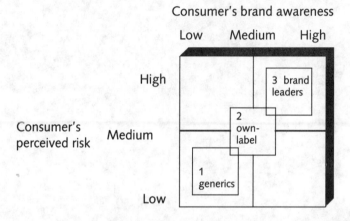

Box 1   This will include products such as sugar, salt and other commodity-type items, for which there tends to be little perceived risk on the part of the consumer and for which consumer brand-awareness is comparatively low. (This equates to the *overall cost leadership/undifferentiated marketing*' box of the Porter matrix.) It would probably be fruitless to enter this market on an own-level basis, unless there were exceptional circumstances which favoured such a decision.

Box 2   This is the danger box and will be full of products which are not outright brand leaders and for which the consumer's perceived risk in making a purchase is not particularly high. Nonetheless, it is here that the retailer's greatest opportunity lies in introducing his own-label brands and competing on price with advertised products. It will be a matter of judgement which products fall into the risky area of box 2.

Box 3   This box is peopled by brand leaders and, often, new products or new concepts. It is here that the true marketing companies sit, like Proctor and Gamble, Mars, Heinz and the like. Such companies have consistently invested in product quality and consumer awareness. Here it is dangerous nonsense for a retailer to convince himself that he can replace brand leaders with own-label products and cheaper substitutes, as the consumer eventually leaves the store for another where they can obtain the brand of their choice. It is not the same for all products, of course, as research at Cranfield has shown. Nonetheless, it behoves the retailer to ascertain what he can and cannot do with many of his brand leaders before reducing their shelf space and believing he can 'get away' with it.

Recently, of course, some top retailers have succeeded in making successful brands out of their own retail names.

On the other hand, those suppliers who have allowed their products to become 'pimply little me-too products' (by replacing above-the-line advertising with below-the-line promotional activities, thus encouraging the consumer to jump from one special offer to another, leading eventually to price wars and product quality deterioration) have no-one but themselves to blame for the consequences. Certainly, it is totally unfair to blame retailers for what such manufacturers see as the misuse of their buying power.

Also, it is clear that for retailers with the right image, it is perfectly feasible for them to join some of the blue chip producers in the top right-hand corner, given appropriate product quality and share-of-consumer mind strategies.

32 Brand strategy

The continued success of a brand strategy can be influenced to a considerable extent by the way the target market is identified and how the brand's differential advantages are perceived.

Differential advantage

	The same	Different
The same	1	2
Different	3	4

Target market

Box 1 Here, it is possible to list hundreds of organizations, like ICI, Cadbury's, Mars, and so on, that trade on their company name and all that it stands for. It is clearly possible to use the company name to imbue a new product in a similar market (i.e. chocolate) with the same company name. Beware, however! (see the note below).

Box 2 Here, the target market is the same, but the differential advantage is different. In such a case, it is possible to use the same company name (e.e. Kelloggs, Anchor, or Cranfield School of Management) in a different product area. An example of this might be Cranfield's chief executive programmes, where the differential advantage for different programmes for CEOs changes, but the target market stays the same.

Box 3 This is a fascinating box, in that the perceived benefits are the same, but the target market is different. Classic examples of this are Mercedes and BMW with their 7, 5 and 3 series. After all, it is still considered the right thing to do to own a BMW!

Box 4 Here, it is essential to have totally separate brand names for each of one's products. Proctor and Gamble, Unilever, BTR, Allied Breweries (Double Diamond, Skol etc.) are classic examples of this.

Note

Please note that the most obvious commercial catastrophes that occur in business are the result of carelessness in the use of *brand names*. Take the classic mistake made by Woolworths. They tried to use their strength to move more up market. Unfortunately, they failed to understand that trying to be in an 'up market' market and a 'down market' market with the same brand name just confuses the consumer. Remember, only a fool would put the name ICI on a face powder or a perfume! Names have very specific connotations, so be very careful before you decide to do range extension or anything like that using the same brand or company name. Use the matrix!

33 Product control

As customers become more demanding about quality, how it is controlled becomes a greater problem for the manufacturer. This matrix looks at products in the light of their quality requirements and control of production.

Quality required

	Low	High
Mainly ours	1	2
Mainly suppliers or sub-contractors	3	4

Control of production

Box 1 Products that fall into this box should present few problems.

Box 2 This box contains the 'headache' products which demand high attention to ensure that quality is maintained. However, the control of production is in your own hands and so quality becomes a 'way of life'.

Box 3 Products in this box can cause minor irritation. Although the quality demands are not high, they are dependent on outside forces. Much time can be wasted on relatively minor issues.

Box 4 This is the 'big-risk' box. The provision of high quality is mainly in the hands of your suppliers or sub-contractors. Hopefully you have chosen them with care, and you do have dual supplies?

Implicit for these products is the need for you and your suppliers to have a good working relationship and for you to have early warning when anything starts to go wrong.

34 Product specification

The specification of a product or service can have serious consequences for how that product/service is produced and how it subsequently performs. The specification can also be the source not only of all the overt costs, but also of many of the hidden ones also. Control over the specification can, therefore, be an important factor in the company's commercial future, as this matrix demonstrates.

Our need to control the specification

	Low	High
High Customer's needs to control the specification	1	2
Low	3	4

Box 1   Here the customer has all the power and it will be in your interest to develop a very close and open working relationship. This 'service' element will doubtless figure high in the customer's choice of supplier.

Box 2   Both parties have an equally high stake in the product specification but a favourable outcome will only result if your negotiating skills are of high quality.

Box 3   The suggestion here is that either the product is largely unspecified, or else it has to conform to an externally imposed specification. One thing is certain, you will not have to spend too much time on customer liaison. However, if a specifying body is involved, maintain good links with it and try to keep abreast of proposed changes.

Box 4   Here you have most freedom. You can alter the design and enhance the product in ways that make sense to you, with minimal interference from the customer. However, don't ever lose sight of the fact that the customer doesn't buy the product, but the *benefits* it provides.

35 Competitor analysis

Competitors can be analysed by considering the relative merits of their customer package, compared with your own, and also the extent to which the reputation they have established makes your commercial success more difficult.

Nature of their offer

	Better 10	Same 5	Worse 0

Their reputation

		Better 10		
			1	2
	Same 5			
			3	4
	Worse 0			

Instructions

Step 1 Make a list of all your main competitors.

Step 2 Consider each competitor in turn and award a score from 0–10 points, according to how their reputation is perceived in the market. Score your own company at 5 and award points either above or below according to each competitor's merits.

Step 3 Again using a 10 point scoring system, consider each competitor's product/service package, relative to your own 5 point score.

Step 4 Plot each competitor on the matrix, using a code letter to identify their position.

Box 1 Competitors in this box offer a better product or service than your company, and have the advantage over you in terms of reputation. Your options are:

- to carry on competing with them at a tremendous disadvantage
- differentiate the product/offer from theirs in some way
- do something about your image and reputation

Box 2 Here, your competitor's output is inferior to yours, but this is cloaked by their better reputation. Your options are:

- to sell much harder, emphasizing differential benefits
- use more advertising and PR to publicize your quality and successes

Box 3   Competitors in this box can be highly dangerous. Their inherently better offer spells trouble for you, and you can bet that they are already scheming of ways to enhance their reputation.

Box 4   Would that all competitors were in this box. Unless they undergo some transformation, they will not give you any sleepless nights.

36 Product and market change

The problem with change is that it can either refer to something quite minor, or to something quite radical. However, from the marketer's point of view there is a tremendous difference between dealing with what is essentially a well-known product, but with the added, wonder ingredient 'X', compared with marketing an entirely new concept.

Similarly, moving into completely new markets brings with it many headaches.

This matrix explores the implications of different degrees of change in both products and markets.

Product

	No change	Modified	Technology change
New market	7 Brand repositioning	8 Product repositioning	9 Innovation
Change marketing mix	4 Re-market	5 Re-launch	6 Conspicuous substitution
No change	1 No change	2 Face lift	3 Inconspicuous substitution

Box 1 With neither the product or market changing, the status quo is maintained.

Box 2 Here there is no change in marketing, but the product is modified. The pressing issues will probably centre around 'increased costs versus benefits' and whether or not the modified product provides greater competitive advantage.

Box 3 Here, because there is no change in marketing, the key issues will focus around manufacturing and handling the new technology and/or materials. Hence there are no fanfares of triumph, the new product creeps quietly on to the scene.

Box 4 Here the product remains the same, but the marketing mix, price, place and promotion are re-blended, thereby constituting a 're-marketing' of the product.

Box 5 Here the issues from boxes 2 and 4 combine and a 're-launch' can be accomplished on the basis of a change of name (if there was one), appearance, costs and the changed marketing mix.

Box 6 Here the changed marketing mix ensures that the new product appears in a more conspicuous manner. All the issues from box 5 will need to be considered, but in addition the new technology and materials will be exercising the company.

Box 7 Here, although the product remains the same, it is now offered a new market. Therefore, in addition to the marketing mix needing to change, there will be new competitors to analyse. Also a new strategy will be required to achieve and maintain a competitive advantage.

Box 8 This box has all the problems of box 7, with the additional factors to take into account, associated with the product modification i.e. appearance, costs, and different features and benefits.

Box 9 Clearly the most complex change of all. Innovation of this magnitude needs to take into account not only the new technology and materials, but also the price, promotion, place, analysis of the new competitors and the total strategic thrust of this initiative.

37 Product design and reliability

The purpose of this matrix is to provide a framework against which product design and reliability can be examined.

Comparative design

	Worse	Better
Comparative reliability Higher	1	2
Lower	3	4

Instructions

Plot your various products on this matrix, having first assessed their merits, in terms of design and reliability, when compared with competing products.

Box 1 Here you score well for reliability, but poorly on design. This being the case, you have two broad options open to you:

- try to improve the design
- try to find a segment of the market where reliability and performance far outweigh appearance

Box 2 Such products ought to be outstanding successes.

Box 3 Any products in this box appear to be 'no-hopers'. You will have to make a tremendous investment in them, in order for them to become competitive. Therefore, unless there are good prospects for market growth, or they are a necessary part of a particular range, get rid of them.

Box 4 Here you outscore competitors on design, but your product is less reliable. In this situation, you have two broad options facing you:

- focus on those markets where your design advantage outweighs reliability
- revise the component specifications, and use value engineering techniques to improve reliability

38 Flexibility

For many companies, the 'service' element of the marketing mix is the area which offers them the greatest chance of differentiating their products or services. One important element of service is the speed at which the company can respond to changing product demands, be they about quantity, quality, or design. This matrix enables the company's response to changing demands to be assessed. In this matrix, 'volatility' means the degree to which the demands of a market change.

Our flequibility to respond

	Low	High
	1	10

	High	10	1	2
Volatility of the markets/ customer groups	Low	1	3	4

Instructions

Step 1 Make a list of the different markets, customer segments and/or important customers.

Step 2 Next, consider each in turn from the point of view of their volatility in terms of product requirement. Allocate each a score between 0–10, where 10 is high.

Step 3 Look down this list with its scores and add another set of scores, again 0–10, but this time reflecting on an honest assessment of your ability to respond to each market/customer group.

Step 4 Plot each market/customer group on the matrix using a code letter to identify each position.

Box 1 This could easily be called the *'missing the bus'* box. The low response flexibility of the company calls into question what it is doing in such a volatile market. Its prospects for success would appear minimal.

Box 2 Here, there is a good match in terms of the company keeping up with the market's fluctuations and change. Such flexibility might see off the challenge from one or two less able competitors over time.

Box 3　This is *'comfy corner'*. There is nothing wrong with being here, but do keep a weather eye open for technological changes, or new entrants, which might have the effect of rocking the boat. Remember, it takes your company longer to adjust to change than others.

Box 4　It could be time to risk flexing the corporate muscles in markets where your ability to respond could bring you higher dividends. At present you can more than cope . . . and have lots of energy to spare.

39 Product life cycle/product development/R&D

This matrix links product development and R&D activity to stages in a product's life (product life cycle). Its purpose is to emphasize the importance of continuous new product development activity, particularly in high growth markets.

Product development activity

		Low	High
Market growth	High	4	3
	Low	1	2

Box 1 In an *embryonic* market, into which you have just launched a new product, your greatest emphasis should be on promotional activity to get the product accepted in the market, so high levels of new product development at this point seem inappropriate, although research and development should obviously continue.

Box 2 In a *mature* or *declining* market, it can often make a lot of sense to focus your R&D activity on minor improvements, whereas it doesn't seem to make sense to spend heavily, especially if a new technology is about to take over. In such a case, spending heavily on the old technology can be a waste of money.

Box 3 Spending relatively heavily on new product development/R&D in a high growth market makes a lot of sense, because in such markets there are often many competitors with very similar products. Anything you can do to differentiate your own by finding better ways of solving the customer's problem should give good returns.

Box 4 There had better be a good reason why your product development activity is low. It could just be complacency, given high sales in a high-growth market. Remember, one day the market will mature, so be sure you are not left behind.

40 Creativity

As product life cycles get ever shorter, it is becoming increasingly important that companies come up with suitable replacement products. This in turn means that companies need to be creative and innovative. The purpose of this matrix is to explore to what extent such requirements are met.

Level of innovation

		Low	Medium	High
Level of creativity	High	3 Self-indulgent creator	6 Fairly innovative creator	9 Winner
	Medium	2 Creative waster	5 Average	8 Fairly creative innovator
	Low	1 Loser	4 Non-creative striver	7 Non-creative copier

To make sense of this matrix, first of all it will be important to define the terms 'creativity' and 'innovation', especially as the former does not appear in most dictionaries.

Creativity is the thinking process that enables us to generate ideas. The ideas themselves can be eccentric or bizarre. *Innovation* is the practical application of such ideas towards meeting the organization's objectives in a more effective way, i.e. innovations must be useful, practical and achieve results.

Instructions

Step 1 Consider your company in terms of how it compares with your main competitors in terms of its record of innovation. Categorize it as low, medium or high.

Step 2 Now get a number of your managers/staff to rate the company in terms of creativity compared with other organizations in which they have worked. From this, admittedly subjective, appraisal, categorize your company as either low, medium or high in creativity.

Note

While innovation can be a matter of fact, creativity is clearly much more difficult to measure objectively.

Boxes 1,2,3 A company which places itself in any of these boxes is destined to be a *loser* in the overall scheme of things. Regardless of its level of creativity, it just cannot produce the practical outcomes which are required.

Box 4 A company here might *just survive*. It is not very creative but manages to introduce some modest innovations, perhaps by mimicking others. We've called it a 'non-creative striver'.

Box 5 This company will *survive* but it will not be outstanding. By placement, it is 'middle of the road'. It is 'average', however you look at it.

Box 6 A company here is *close to being a winner*. Its high level of creativity does not quite find its full translation into innovation. For this reason we've labelled it 'fairly innovative creator'.

Box 7 A company here will *survive* on the basis of its high level of innovation. However, what stops it from being a winner is the lack of originality in its innovations – they are likely to be incremental steps, rather than quantum leaps, and possibly copies of other companies.

Box 8 Here is a *successful* company that only just falls short of being a winner by dint of its relative lack of creativity.

Box 9 Companies here have every likelihood of being *winners*. They have at their disposal a reservoir of creativity, matched with an ability to convert ideas into practical results.

Notes

From the above analysis, it can be seen that creativity is the 'seed corn' of innovation. If a company is not naturally creative, it can make use of creative 'idea-generating techniques', thereby improving its chances of success. There are several books devoted to 'creative thinking'. One we would recommend is *The Creative Gap* by Simon Majaro (Longman, Harlow, 1988).

41   Types of product/service

Products and services can be differentiated by their functionality or by their image. Anything is better than a 'pimply little me-too product', but the safest bet is to combine the best of both worlds.

Image

	Differ- entiated	Undiffer- entiated
Differentiated	1	2
Undifferentiated	4	3

Content of product/service

Box 1   Here we have a very *exclusive* product, not easily matched by competitors, because both the image and content of the product have been cleverly differentiated.

Box 2   Here, the product is *special*, because of its differentiated content, but has no image differentiation.

Box 3   Products in this box are clearly *standard*, me-toos.

Box 4   Potentially a me-too product, but the essential difference is that it has been *augmented* by developing a differentiated image for it. This clearly gives it greater market potential over standard products.

42 Product/market profitability

Research has shown (product impact of market strategies, PIMS) that there is a clear relationship between profitability, market share and product quality. In this context, product quality means not just the tangible product, but the quality of the total offer or relationship. If customers perceive this as being of high quality, they are prepared to pay more for it. The purpose of this matrix is to explore this relationship.

Product quality

	High	Low
High	4	3
Low	1	2

Market share

Instructions

Step 1 Consider each product in terms of its quality requirements and market share. Allocate scores of 0–10 for each of these dimensions, using criteria that make sense for your business.

Step 2 Plot each product on the matrix, using a code letter to identify the product's position.

Box 1 Low market share and high product quality. The profitability of companies in this box are around 20 per cent (measured in terms of return on investment). This is because, although the company has a low market share, customers are prepared to pay for a product which they perceive as being of good quality.

Box 2 This is the worst box of all because the company has both a low perceived product quality and a low market share (the two things are obviously connected!). Profitability for companies in this box is generally very low. If you are in this box, you should seriously consider closing down and putting your money in the bank – you'd make more money!

Box 3 These low product quality/high market share companies generally manage to make about the same amount of relative profit as companies in box 1 (i.e. around 20 per cent). These profits almost certainly result from low costs as a result of economies of scale. Products here are often in a mass market and are possibly quite difficult to differentiate in any way, and the main purchase criterion is price. Nonetheless, it's still quite good business.

Box 4   Obviously the best box of all, combining as it does both high perceived product quality with high market share. Companies with products in this box average around 40 per cent return on investment! Think about this very carefully as it's obviously the place to be.

4 Customer

43 Segmentation matrix

The basis for market segmentation can be critical to the subsequent ways a company mobilizes its resources. Sometimes segmentation can be achieved by focusing on the market itself, and sometimes by focusing on product usage. Equally, there are differences between industrial and consumer markets.

This matrix demonstrates how these factors combine, and what the implications might be regarding the sort of information required to form the basis of segmentation.

```
                          Main focus on

                       Market    Products
                     ┌─────────┬─────────┐
                     │         │         │
        Industrial   │    1    │    2    │
                     │         │         │
Type of market       ├─────────┼─────────┤
                     │         │         │
        Consumer     │    3    │    4    │
                     │         │         │
                     └─────────┴─────────┘
```

Box 1 Here we are looking at an industrial market, focusing on the characteristics of the market. In these circumstances segmentation could be achieved on the basis of:

- standard industrial classification
- geographical location
- company size
- make-up of the decision making unit (DMU)
- main technology etc. etc.

Box 2 Here the industrial market is considered through analysing the products it consumes. Thus segmentation could be the basis of:

- usage patterns
- distribution costs
- service levels
- unitization
- accessories/range, etc. etc.

Box 3 Here segmentation in the consumer market might be considered in terms of market indicators such as:

- socio-economic groups
- customer life style patterns
- demographics, etc. etc.

Box 4   Here segmentation might be considered in terms of:

- consumption patterns
- features and benefits
- innovation theory etc. etc.

44　Customer segmentation

Customer segmentation is at the heart of all successful marketing initiatives. However, the way segmentation is done can depend on a number of different factors, as this matrix shows.

The successful company chooses a segmentation approach which enables them to exploit their distinctive competence, thereby establishing a competitive advantage in the market.

Basis of segmentation	Factors to consider
What is bought?	Volume Price Outlets Physical features/ characteristics
Who buys?	Customers or consumers Demographics Socio-economic Brand loyalty Personality types Life styles
Why?	Needs Benefits Attitudes Perceptions Preferences Motivation

Note

Customers make the purchase, whereas consumers actually use the product or service. Sometimes the customer and consumer are the same person, but often they are not. This distinction can be very important for some types of business. It could entail different strategies being devised for each group.

45   Product life cycle/customer's loyalty

This matrix considers the value of investing time and effort into winning customer loyalty, against a backdrop of varying levels of market growth.

Customer loyalty

	Low	High
High	2	3
Low	1	4

Market growth

Box 1   Unless you are in an embryonic market or are a specialist company, it would seem to be an expensive luxury to work at building customer loyalty in such a low-growth market.

Box 2   Clearly, there can be a long-term advantage in *developing* customer loyalty for those who fall into this box. So don't delay, get cracking on it!

Box 3   The success box, where you can reap the rewards of customer loyalty, but don't get complacent, you will need to *work to maintain* such loyalty.

Box 4   Some customers are surprisingly loyal to their suppliers. If you have their trust and support, even in a low-growth market (as illustrated by this box), try *not to* do anything *to lose it*. But beware of spending too much in mature markets.

46 Customer targeting

Successful companies realize that they have to target their resources on those areas of business from which they are likely to see the best returns. This matrix provides one method of targeting customers.

Customer's attitude/
loyalty to your company

	Good	Bad
High	4	3
Low	1	2

Available sales potential

Instructions

For the purposes of this matrix, it will be necessary to consider all of your current customers in terms of:

- current level of sales
- potential sales over the next three years
- your assessment of their loyalty/attitude to your company

Box 1 Here, list all customers who like you, but who have little potential for increased sales. These are likely to be either small customers or large customers whose business you already have. Clearly, this is not an area where it is worth devoting too many resources. Consider ways in which you can minimize communications to them, especially expensive sales visits, and yet still maintain their favourable attitude to your company.

Box 2 Here, list all customers who don't like you and who have little potential. We suggest you don't waste too much of your time on them!

Box 3 Here, list those customers with lots of potential, but who just don't like you. You must work out whether it is worth dedicating your resources to making their attitude more favourable towards you. Perhaps it would be worth targeting a few potentially valuable customers in this box, in order to learn just how easy (or difficult) it is to change attitudes.

Box 4   This is the best box of all and is the one in which you should list those customers with lots of potential and who like you. Obviously, this box should be a prime target for your sales and promotional effort. Work hard to maintain a positive attitude and loyalty from these customers.

47 Propensity to buy

Buying decisions are influenced by many factors. However, research has shown that two of the most potent forces are the nature of the product itself, and the extent to which the customer 'trusts' the seller. The purpose of this matrix is to illustrate how these factors relate, and what the implications might be for your company.

You will have to use your judgement and experience about your particular business to decide where you position your company on this matrix. It might be possible to be in two positions. For example, you may be largely unknown as a company, with a range of 'me-too' products, but you may also have one or two unique ones.

```
                          Our product
                      Me-too      Unique

        Well-known       1           2
Customer's
knowledge of
our company
        Unknown          3           4
```

Box 1 Although you might be well-known, your product or service is to all intents and purposes the same as many others on the market. Therefore, your degree of success operating in this box is likely to depend largely on the skills of your sales force and the general promotion of your product.

Box 2 If you are in this happy situation, you've got it made. A research study made into the buying decisions by one large company found that the decision to buy automatically resulted 90 per cent of the time.

Box 3 Almost the opposite was found to be true here. A 'not to buy' decision resulted 90 per cent of the time. If you have placed your company in this box, you have got problems. Probably your first step will be to differentiate your product, if you can, so that it becomes more attractive for a specific sub-group of customers. Life is not going to be easy.

Box 4 It has been found that customers are suspicious about dealing with companies about whom they know little, even if they have first-class products. As with box 1, success seems to depend on the impact that sales and advertising make on the situation. It is here that you will have to focus your efforts.

48 Customer portfolio

This matrix plots the frequency of purchase of customers against the degree of loyalty to the supplier. Frequency of purchase denotes the number of occasions on which an order is placed. Loyalty to supplier denotes the tendency to lose customers. The causes could be, aggressive marketing by competitors; price rises; poor customer service; neglect; and so on. The matrix can be used to analyse the current customer mix in order to allocate promotional effort and, if necessary, market research effort.

Loyalty to us

	High	Low
High	4	3
Low	1	2

Purchasing frequency

Box 1 These customers have a high loyalty to you, but their purchasing frequency is low, denoting that they are probably *new customers*. Here, the task is one of building the relationship by providing high levels of service in order to ensure that repeat business is assured.

Box 2 Customers in this box may well have made '*one-off*' purchases, for reasons best known to them. If the potential business seems to be worth it, efforts should be made to build the relationship. If such efforts seem in vain, let these customers go.

Box 3 Customers in this category are likely to be '*lost customers*'. Find out why! There is usually a good reason why customers turn '*traitor*'.

Box 4 Obviously, the best customers of all! Do everything in your power to keep these customers satisfied. They really are '*angels*', so look after them well.

49 Customer relationship (1)

This matrix is adapted from the work of Joe Luft and Harry Ingham, who developed a matrix about personal relationships in the late 1960s, popularly known as the Johari Window. This adaptation helps us to understand what strategies might be most appropriate to improve relations with each individual customer, or groups of customers.

Our company

	What we know about us	What we don't know
What they know about us	1	2
What they don't know about us	3	4

Customer(s)

Instructions

Take each individual customer, or important groups of customers, in turn and consider the nature of your relationship with them, in the context of this matrix.

Box 1 This is the only area where openness and trust can be established, because 'what they see is what they get'. This is the *business arena*.

Box 2 No matter how good we might think we are at managing customer relations, we can never experience what it is like dealing with ourselves. (Although sometimes a salutary lesson can be learned by 'phoning in as a potential customer and seeing how your call is handled!) This is our *blind spot* and it will always remain so unless we attempt to get feedback via questionnaires and discussions with customers.

Box 3 Just like people, companies also know things about themselves which they choose to keep private. This is our secret world, or *façade*. Unfortunately, we often keep too much to ourselves and do not broadcast enough about the company's strengths and success stories. As a result, we remain remote and mysterious.

Box 4 This is the genuine *unknown* and perhaps represents the hidden potential in the relationship.

Note

The significant thing about this matrix is that it is not static, but developing, as, indeed, anything representing a relationship ought to be. So, when a new customer begins to do business with us, the matrix will look something like this.

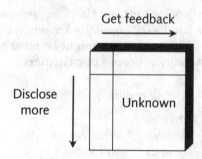

In other words, the business arena is rather small and the relationship is dominated by the relatively huge unknown. In order to develop a better customer relationship, it will be necessary for us to disclose much more about our company, thus reducing the facade. Also, it will be valuable for us to find out what the customer expects of us, and the extent to which we live up to those expectations.

Clearly, there needs to be a natural pace at which this is done, and both the pace, and the strategies for opening up the arena, need to be given serious consideration. Many companies are not equally skilled in both these areas of disclosure and receiving feedback. Indeed, the prospect of receiving genuine feedback from their customers is something many seek to avoid.

50 Customer relationship (2)

This matrix provides a variation on the preceding one, using slightly different parameters. However, its purpose is the same . . . to focus attention on how well you relate to customers.

This matrix can also be used for developing relationships with distributors or other channel intermediaries.

What customers know about us

	Little	A lot
A lot	1	2
A little	3	4

What we know about the customer

Instructions

To use this matrix you need to allocate your individual customers (certainly your major ones) to the appropriate boxes.

Box 1 This could be termed the *'coy'* box. Here you are saying that you know a lot about the customer – which makes good business sense. However, the customer doesn't know much about you. This can pose something of a dilemma, because it suggests that:

- you have something to hide (which might be true!)
- you enjoy being mysterious (which can be self-defeating when it comes to developing trust and confidence with the customer)

Box 2 This is the *'open'*, *'what you see is what you get'* box. Ultimately, it is the only box which provides a basis for a strong and lasting relationship with a customer.

Box 3 This is the *'strangers'* box. Unless your business is one where it is not important to develop a good relationship with your customer, you have a lot of work on your hands.

Box 4 This is the *'very brave'*, or *'very stupid'* box. If everything there is to know about your company is above reproach, you have no problems. Otherwise, you are in effect, giving all the power to the customer. Since you know little about the customer, you are working blindfold.

51 Influencing the customer

When a customer makes a decision to purchase, there is often more than one person involved. For example, the acquisition of some production plant is likely to involve the managing director, production director, technical director, financial director, and maybe one or two others. This group would be called the decision making unit (DMU).

Clearly, the purchase of low-cost items is often delegated to just one person. Even so, in a majority of other buying situations, some form of DMU will usually be found. This matrix considers how customers might best be influenced.

Number of people in
decision making unit

	Few	Many
Many	1	2
Few	3	4

Number of
customer contacts

Box 1 In the circumstances outlined by this box, the company has more than enough contacts. This can either add to the communication – or to the confusion. It is essential to establish who, out of these many contacts, constitutes the DMU. Special attention should then be given to these individuals, in terms of satisfying their particular requirements during the transactions.

Box 2 As in box 1, it will be essential to determine who forms the DMU. Research has shown that, while the number of people in the DMU increases with size of company and/or size of the purchase, rarely are more than two contacts properly cultivated. This could leave a company extremely vulnerable.

Box 3 Are the few contacts the right contacts? The chances are that they are not, because most contact with customers tends to be at lower levels in the organization, whereas the purchasing decisions are invariably made by those in the higher levels.

Box 4 This has the makings of a disaster. By not having the opportunity to influence all members of the DMU, the chances of getting a favourable outcome are greatly diminished.

52 Influencing the decision making unit

The previous matrix discussed the concept of the buying decision being made by a decision making unit. This matrix extends this idea and provides an opportunity to plan who in the DMU needs to be influenced in which way, and at what phase of the buying process.

Buy phase	Individual members of DMU (by name or position)						
1 Recognizes need or problem and has ideas about what form the general solution should take							
2 Works at characteristics and quality of what is required							
3 Prepares detailed specification							
4 Searches to locate potential suppliers							
5 Analyses and compares competing offers							
6 Selects the most advantageous offer							
7 Places order							
8 Checks that product/service meets expectations in use.							

Instructions

The vertical axis of the matrix lists the phases that typify all buying decisions. The horizontal axis provides spaces for the individual members of the DMU (of a particular customer organization) to be listed.

Each of these people will in all probability take some of the following factors into consideration as they play their part in the buying decision. However, these factors will be of varying importance to different members of the DMU, *and* at different buy phases.

Influencing factors

- price
- performance characteristics
- delivery
- back-up service
- reliability of supplies
- design
- experiences with competitors
- guarantees and warranties
- payment terms, credit and discount
- past purchases/relationship
- image, prestige, etc.
- add any other factor

To use the matrix, indicate which factors (by using the numbers designated to them) are relevant to each member of the DMU at each stage of the buying process.

Having done this, your task will now be to plan how each of these people can receive the appropriate information, which communication methods will be used, and importantly, the timing of these communications.

53 Consumer decision-making

This matrix considers some of the factors which influence consumer decision-making. It is important for marketers to know in which boxes their products and services are positioned, because it has clear implications for the nature of support they need to provide. This can be in terms of advertising message, point of sale materials, brochures and even the training of sales staff.

Importance of purchase
to consumer

	High	Low
Significant	1	2
Minor	3	4

Perceived brand
differences

Instructions

This is a conceptual framework and does not require any additional data.

Box 1 This describes a high level of importance attributed to the purchase, and significant perceived brand differences. For example, a housewife wishing to buy a new washing machine will be very concerned that she makes the right decision. It is very important to her, because it is central to the way she organizes things around the home. If she perceives significant brand differences among the appliances on offer, then it is likely that she will spend a lot of time researching and comparing their various features and benefits.

Both of these factors, high importance and significant perceived differences, have the effect of *extending the consumer decision-making process*.

Box 2 Here, the importance of the purchase to the consumer is low, for example, in the case of buying groceries. Although there might be significant perceptions of brand differences (e.g. own-label versus brand leader), the relatively low level of importance does *not delay the buying decision unduly*.

Box 3 Here, the importance to the consumer is high, but relatively small differences are perceived among competing brands. While this might lead to an element of procrastination on behalf of the consumer, all he or she really *requires* is *confirmation* that, whatever their purchase decision, they are making the correct choice.

Box 4   Here, both of the factors under consideration are at a low level. In such circumstances, the consumer is likely to make a *rapid purchasing decision* based predominantly on previous experience. Impulse buying might be encouraged with a suitable eye-catching gimmick.

5 Sales

5 Sales

54　Sales person performance

Successful sales people do not trust to luck, they work hard for their success. They try to maximize their time in front of potential customers, and strive to be as professional as they can when doing so. This matrix provides a framework against which the performance of all sales people can be evaluated.

Box 1 This sales person is getting to see about the right number of potential customers, but since the quality of the calls is poor, it is unlikely that good results will be achieved. Normally, such a person has to be a candidate for training and coaching.

    There is an exception to this diagnosis, as the next matrix demonstrates. If the product is well-known and highly promoted, it will virtually sell itself.

Box 2 This person ought to be one of your stars. If good results are not being achieved then perhaps there is something wrong with your product/service in terms of how it compares with competing offers.

Box 3 Anyone in this box is a pretty hopeless case. Sack the sales manager, for it's hardly fair to blame the sales person for the poor performance.

Box 4 This person is either spending too long on sales visits, or else needs to reconsider how he/she tackles territory planning (see matrix). A third possibility is that this person's sales area is so spread out geographically, that it is impossible to make the required number of calls. In this case, the area needs adjusting. People in this box have the potential to be successful, but just need some guidance.

Note

Here are some ideas for achieving improvements:

Increased quality through

- presentation skills
- product/service knowledge
- benefit analysis and explanation
- use of visual aids
- better promotional materials
- sales skills e.g. overcoming objections and closing

Increased quantity through

- better territory allocation
- route planning
- work habits
- record keeping
- administrative back-up
- time management

55   Sales person remuneration

It is a perennial problem about how best to remunerate sales staff. Results ought to bring their own rewards . . . but do they? Some products or services almost sell themselves, so how should the sales person be remunerated in these situations? The purpose of this matrix is to illustrate where sales people have to work hardest, and how they might be best motivated, in terms of how they are paid.

Product/brand advantage

	High	Low
High	2	3
Low	1	4

Promotion of
brand/product

Box 1   Here, the product has lots of advantages over competing products, but isn't very well-known, because it isn't promoted heavily. Therefore, there is a real selling job to be done and a remuneration package of a salary and bonus/commission makes a lot of sense.

Box 2   Here, the product has many advantages and is heavily promoted. This makes the sales person's task relatively simple, and so it would be worthwhile to be set additional objectives for such sales calls. A straight salary structure is probably appropriate here.

Box 3   Here the product receives heavy promotion, but is physically little different from competitive products. As in box 1, this means there is a formidable selling job to be done. Again, a mix of salary and bonus/commission would seem to be appropriate.

Box 4   A real sales person's paradise! Also a big challenge. Here, not only is the product not well-known, but it has few advantages over competitive products. A commission-based remuneration scheme often provides the added incentive for this difficult task. Excellent sales people get rich here. Conversely, the also-rans do nothing but moan about how poorly they are paid.

56 Features and benefits

All products and services have features which are intended to provide customer benefits. Thus, the customer doesn't buy the product, but the value benefits which that product supplies.

There is the well known story of the customer who buys a drill, not because he loves drills, but because he needs to make a hole. If there were other, cheaper, more efficient ways of making holes, then our drill manufacturer would be in trouble.

Intellectually, the concept of features and benefits is readily understood. In practice, however, we have found that some sales people do not always discuss features and benefits. This matrix illustrates the consequences of different types of sales interviews, and suggests remedial action.

	Features	
	Not mentioned	Mentioned
Benefits Not mentioned	1	2
Mentioned	3	4

Box 1 If the sales person doesn't talk about features or benefits, what is discussed? This person is to sales, what Billy Bunter would be to ballet dancing!

Box 2 Here, the sales person is an enthusiast for the product. There is nothing that isn't known about it, including how it was made. Unfortunately, this salesperson doesn't realize that this approach leaves the customer thinking 'so what!' He or she must learn to see the product through the customer's eyes and be more sensitive to ways in which it will benefit the customer. One way of doing this would be to draw up a benefit analysis sheet (see below).

Box 3 This sales person might be successful, but grabbing benefits out of thin air, and not relating them to features, is like a conjuror pulling rabbits out of a hat. He or she would be more effective if they described a feature of the product and then linked it to a benefit. An expression like . . . 'which means that' . . . can often form a superb bridge. For example, 'this part is made of diamond, which means that it will never wear out and the life of the unit exceeds all others on the market'.

Box 4 This person knows how to use features and benefits. Get him or her to show the others how it's done.

Note

The text in box 2 referred to benefit analysis. Here is an example of how such an analysis might be set out.

Benefit analysis sheet

Customer ....

Product/services required ....

Appeal	Features	Advantages	Benefits	Proof
What issues are of particular concern to this customer?	What features of the product/service can illustrate these issues?	What advantages do these features provide?	What tangible benefits can be expressed to give customer appeal?	What evidence can be provided to back up claims that benefits do result?
e.g. cost, reliability, safety etc.	What are they? How do they work?	i.e. what do they do for the customer?	i.e. what does the customer get that he/she needs?	

57 Selling style

A lot of work has been done examining the issue of 'selling style'. Two factors have been shown to have considerable bearing on the way a salesperson behaves when with a customer. These are the degree of concern for making a sale, and the degree of concern for developing or maintaining a relationship with that customer.

This matrix looks at how these two factors can combine.

	Concern for sale	
	Low	High
High	1	4
Low	2	3

Concern for sale — Low / High (top)

Concern for the relationship with customer — High / Low (left)

Box 1 This selling style values the customer relationship very highly and is combined with a low concern for making the sale. Such a sales person is clearly not going to be very forceful and is likely to respond to the customer's every whim. This sales person will have great trouble overcoming objections or closing the sale, and would hate the thought of the customer saying no. Such a style is best employed on after-sales service calls, or dealing with customer complaints.

Box 2 This style is pretty apathetic and not at all successful. This sales person will probably work to the book and do just enough to get by. He or she will always need to be pushed to produce extra. The only way in which such people might be employed is in straight order-taking circumstances.

Box 3 This is the 'toughie' selling style. Such a sales person will try to take complete control of the sales interview and show little interest in the concerns of the customer. Everything is subordinate to that one objective ... to get the sale. This apparently commendable attitude often proves to be self-defeating, because without establishing a relationship with the customer, there is little warmth or trust developed, and sales are not achieved. However, such a selling style can be successful in situations where long-term relationships with the customer are not required e.g. door-to-door selling.

Box 4 This is the true professional, who never loses sight of the objective of the sales interview, but who also realizes the importance of building a relationship with the customer.

58 Sales call categorization

Just as companies have to ration their resources, so do sales staff. The cost of having sales people in the field is so high that it is essential that they direct their attentions to situations with the best prospects of success.

This matrix illustrates how this can be done and therefore can be a valuable aid for better territory planning.

Size of existing or potential business

		Large	Medium	Small
Sales person's relationship with customer	Friendly	1	2	3
	Middle of the road	4	5	6
	Hostile	7	8	9

Instructions

Encourage your sales staff to plot each of their customers on this matrix, using a code letter, to designate within which box each customer falls.

Box 1 Most sales people have a proclivity for calling frequently on large customers who give them a friendly reception, as suggested by this box. However, the fact that they have already established such a good relationship, suggests that they could in fact cut down on the number of visits to companies in this box. They should adopt a maintenance strategy, keeping in contact by 'phone or letter between visits.

Box 2 Much the same arguments apply here as with box 1. Adopt a maintenance strategy.

Box 3 Here, relationships are good, but since the sales potential is so low, companies here should receive minimum attention, consistent with the company's marketing objectives.

Box 4 Here, there is a large sales potential, but an indifferent relationship. Here it is worth the effort of visiting more frequently in order to establish a better relationship with these customers. The potential results would justify this investment of time. (The time savings have, of course, come from reduced visits to companies in boxes 1, 2, 3, 6 and 9).

Box 5 Another set of companies that are worth investing in, second only to box 4.

Box 6 Here, minimum attention is required, consistent with your company's goals.

Box 7 Here, alternative strategies should be attempted to overcome the hostility. The high potential makes this worth trying, even on just a limited number of these companies.

Box 8 As for box 7.

Box 9 Don't bother with these companies.

59   Measuring sales performance

An individual sales person's performance is dependent on the objectivity, or quantification of targets. Without a tangible target, there is no reference point against which to measure.

Equally, it is essential that some form of reporting system is in place. This needs to be capable of giving an accurate picture of what is actually happening. This matrix explores how these two factors can combine.

Objectivity of target

	Vague	Clear
Good	1	2
Poor	3	4

Adequacy of reporting system

Box 1   Your superb reporting system is being done a disservice by the vague nature of the sales targets which are set. In trying to measure sales performance, you are trying to make bricks without straw. Get those targets sorted out! Some suggestions about types of quantitative targets are given below.

Box 2   Your finger is clearly on the pulse and you have up-to-date and objective information regarding how the sales staff are performing.

Box 3   You are stumbling around in a mist here. You have nothing which can give you any kind of control over what is going on. The sooner you start sorting something out, the better it will be.

Box 4   You are setting objective targets, it seems. Yet you don't have adequate systems to give you feedback on how they are met. Surely, it makes sense to improve the reporting system? A situation like this ought to be easy to remedy.

Quantitative objective for sales persons

The principal objectives are usually concerned with the following measures:

- how much to sell (in value or volume terms)
- what to sell (product mix)
- where to sell (customers that figure in marketing plan)
- desired profit contribution
- selling costs (against budget)

There can, of course, be a number of other types of objectives, including the following:

- number of point-of-sale displays organized
- number of letters written to prospects
- number of reports submitted
- number of trade meetings held
- use of sales aids in presentations
- number of service calls made
- number of customer complaints
- safety record/safe driving mileage
- number of training meetings conducted for customers
- competitive activity/market condition reports.

60 Sales calls and orders

To some extent, it is possible to build up an arithmetical model of a company's sales activities and their effectiveness. X number of customer contacts leads to Y number of enquiries. In turn, this leads to w number of sales proposals being put to customers, which result in z number of concrete orders.

The extent to which these subsequent numbers decrease from x, at each phase of the customer contact, is some measure of the sales person's selling effectiveness.

This matrix looks at the start and finish of the process – sales calls and orders received.

Number of sales calls

	Low	High
High	1	2
Low	3	4

Number of orders received

Instructions

Consider each of your sales persons in turn. Assess their individual inputs (in terms of sales visits) and outputs (orders received). Using this information, locate each sales person on the matrix, using an initial or code letter to enable you to distinguish one from another.

Box 1 This person is magic, converting so many calls into orders . . . or is it that he/she has all the long-standing, friendly customers in their sales area? If not, probably everyone could learn from finding out what this sales person actually does at sales interviews. While there is a temptation to accept this obvious level of success, just think what the results could be if the number of sales calls was increased, even by a modest amount!

Box 2 This box supports the thesis that success is 90 per cent perspiration and 10 per cent inspiration. Give the sales manager a bonus.

Box 3 Unless there are extenuating circumstances . . . and it's difficult to think what they could be, fire the sales manager. This sales person is costing you a fortune, swanning around the country.

Box 4 Surely, you haven't got anyone in this box! If you have, it must be a case of nepotism. The best thing you can do is put this person on a commission-only remuneration package.

61 Sales person autonomy

As life in general has become more hurried and complex, so have many sales situations. However, for reasons best known to themselves, many companies do not give their sales people the level of autonomy they need to deal with the situations they face. This matrix examines the consequences of this.

Complexity of the sales situation

	Low	High
High	1	2
Low	3	4

Freedom of action given to sales person

Box 1   Be careful, this sales person has been given a lot of autonomy in what is a fairly straightforward sales situation. Make sure that he or she doesn't start to self-actualize, because they are getting bored.

Box 2   In highly complex sales situations, the sales person will need to have a high level of autonomy. Nothing can be more galling for the customer than to hear repeatedly, 'I've got to check that with my manager'. On the other hand, you, in turn, must be certain that the sales person is sufficiently experienced and mature to handle this level of autonomy.

Box 3   Probably a reasonable match, taking the circumstances into account.

Box 4   This is the equivalent of sending your infantry into battle with rifles but no bullets. Don't you trust them, or are your sales people incompetent? Either way, you have a management problem on your hands. A fresh look at your recruitment and training policy might give you some clues about where to take action.

62   Sales person personality

This matrix is included to provide a little light relief. However, be warned, there is often much truth hidden in jest.

Intelligence

	Clever	Stupid
Lazy	1	3
Hard working	2	4

Application

Box 1   A clever sales person, with the unfortunate characteristic of laziness. A pity, but just about acceptable.

Box 2   A clever and hard-working person. Let's have a lot more like this!

Box 3   This person is stupid, but has the advantage of being lazy!

Box 4   This is the worst possible scenario. This person is stupid, but works hard! They have a boss who makes the situation worse by encouraging them to double the chaos and upset twice as many customers each day!

Note

The perceptive reader will readily see how box 4 people would fit well into the management style of box 3 in matrix 2!

63 Sales person training priorities

This matrix helps to make decisions about which sales people are the ones most deserving of a share of the sales training budget.

Breadth of experience and skills

	Narrow	Wide
High	1	2
Low	3	4

Level of commitment/motivation for selling

Instructions

Roughly position each sales person on this matrix. Clearly, your choice is going to be largely subjective . . . so why not get one or two of your colleagues to do this same task?

We find that when such results are compared, there is often a high level of correlation. This suggests that it is possible to use this matrix with some confidence.

Box 1 Sales people in this box are highly committed to selling (as opposed to seeing it as just a job), but have only a narrow breadth of experience. These are your *potentials*, and are worth investing in, with training. Their willingness to succeed makes them the sort of people who will readily learn, and put their learning into practice.

Box 2 These are the *performers*. They are the people who get results. At first sight it could appear that people in this box don't need training, but they do. It should be your *first priority* to see that these people are always on top of their game. Because of their attitude, they do not see training to be demeaning.

Box 3 These are your *passengers*. Money invested in training for this group will, in all probability, be wasted.

Box 4 These are your *possibles*. They have the necessary experience, but their lack of commitment stops them from firing on all cylinders. They always seem to need someone to push and cajole them into action. For this reason, investment in this group is always questionable.

64 Sales managers

Managers, by and large, influence others on the basis of either their organizational power (the job title and job description), or their personal power (personality, charisma and competence). Equally, a manager's ability to influence others is to a large extent governed by the contact time spent with them. This is the thinking behind this particular matrix.

Influences staff on basis of

	Organiz- ational power	Competence
In office	1	2
In field	3	4

Usually to be found

Box 1 Here is your bureaucrat manager who enjoys the trappings of power. He/she sits in the office, sending out memos and pouring over sales plans, always contriving to look busy. In the context of doing this, he/she will come up with some brilliant ideas (in their eyes). They get such ideas introduced by bullying and pulling rank. When, as they usually do, the ideas fail to work, then look out! A scapegoat (not them) has to be found.

Box 2 At first sight, this box seems similar to box 1, but instead of being a 'desk jockey' like the above, this manager is competent. He/she will have a finger on the pulse of what is going on and conduct affairs with a light, but confident touch. Even so, it would be useful for this manager to get out into the field more often.

Box 3 This manager causes even more problems than his/her office-bound equivalent. He/she throws weight around in the field, trying to impress customers, but only succeeding in belittling the field sales force. Since each foray into the field is perceived as a 'royal visit', subordinates are uncomfortable and do their best to keep the truth of what is going on carefully hidden.

Box 4 This manager is competent and close to the action. As a result, he/she can see what is going on and coach or counsel their subordinates, thereby achieving even better results. There are not all that many managers of this type around, yet, to be successful, companies need them.

65 Purchase decision makers

This matrix provides a useful guide regarding who might be involved in the purchasing decision in a commercial setting.

Commercial risk

	Low	High
High	1	2
Low	3	4

Complexity of product or service

Box 1 Here, the commercial risk is low, while the complexity of the product or service is high. In these circumstances the principal decision maker is likely to be the purchasing company's functional specialist, i.e. the person most conversant with the technology of the impending purchase.

Box 2 Here, both the complexity and the risk are at high levels. For these reasons, a number of key people throughout the purchasing company will have to be satisfied that the purchase will be beneficial. Therefore the decision making unit (DMU) is likely to be large.

Box 3 With both the complexity and risk at a low level, most organizations would leave the decision to buy to the purchasing manager.

Box 4 In this box, the complexity is low, but the commercial risk high. Therefore, the purchasing decision will be likely to be made principally by the purchasing manager and the company's senior financial staff.

6 Pricing

66 Product life cycle and price

This matrix describes the different pricing strategies that need to be used as a product goes through its life cycle.

Box 1 Here, you have a low-growth market and a high price. This could be because the market is embryonic and because you are dealing with a new product. If this is the case, beware of creating a price umbrella for potential entrants. This represents a price 'skimming' policy and is only really valid if you have a long technological lead. But even here it's worth considering whether a lower price would lead to quicker market penetration and lower costs. If the market is mature or even in decline, a high-price policy is probably acceptable, as long as you are not 'milking' the product and giving up future profits for profits today by allowing your competitors to grow at your expense.

Box 2 Here, the very opposite of the comments given above in relation to box 1 apply. A low price in a low-growth market could obviously be the right policy, but again, beware of wasting money on low prices in a mature market in order to gain market share. A more appropriate strategy would probably be to maintain your market position.

Box 3 A low-price policy in a high-growth market could well help gain market penetration, hence market share, with all the attendant benefits of reducing costs and improving margins. However, with a high quality product, the price has to be consistent with the product's image, so care is needed here.

Box 4 A high-price policy in a high-growth market could well be the wrong way to go (but not necessarily so), and often conflicts with market share growth aspirations. As ever, it's comparatively easy to make good profits in a high-growth market, and it can be very tempting to adopt a high-price policy in relation to competitors.

Remember, however, that price and market share are sometimes related, so be careful not to lose market share in order to maximize profitability. It's a wonderful feeling now, but don't forget the longer term situation as the market matures and as the growth rate declines. Could you cope with falling sales and falling profits?

67   Retail pricing

Pricing is something of an art, rather than a science. Many factors come into play when pricing decisions have to be made. Not least among the factors to consider are those provided by this matrix.

Consumer price awareness

	Low	High
High	2 'High' price	4
Low	3	1 'Low' price

Actual price charged

Box 1   Here, the customer is highly aware of minor differences in price. Often, products in this box will be high-turnover branded goods. For example, a dog food might fall into this category. It would clearly be dangerous not to price it keenly.

Box 2   Here, the consumer price awareness is low and, as a result, it is possible to price comparatively highly.

Box 3   To charge low prices here is really equivalent to shooting oneself in the foot. The low price awareness gives you scope to experiment with higher prices.

Box 4   To charge high prices to high price aware customers is also a dubious policy. The only exceptions to this comment would be special circumstances, such as a late opening store, or a speciality store, or the equivalent, where an added service can be seen to justify the high price.

68 Pricing strategy

Whenever costs can be reduced, there is a prospect of improving the profit margins on products or services. However, most marketers are aware that costs are not everything. Customers are nearly always prepared to pay higher prices for products if, by doing so, they receive higher value benefits.

This matrix explores some of the possibilities which exist and which can influence a pricing strategy.

Opportunity for cost reduction

		Low	High
	High	4	3
Opportunity for value enhancement	Low	1	2
		Low	High

Instructions

Consider each of your products (or services) in turn, in terms of the axes of this matrix. Use your judgement to place each product in one of the four boxes provided.

Box 1 In this situation, the industry price will follow costs and in particular, the costs of the price leader. This can be labelled as a 'follow-the-leader strategy'.

Box 2 Here, price is set low by the early entrant to gain advantage of the price-sensitive market and thus gain market share and lower costs. This can be labelled a 'penetration strategy'.

Box 3 Through a combination of high added value plus low costs, these companies are able to bring down the price 'umbrella' and shake out the less innovative or higher cost competitors. This strategy can be labelled 'price leadership'.

Box 4 Under a 'skimming strategy', it is assumed that the cost reduction opportunities are low, hence a less steep experience curve.

69 The brand/commodity slide

Price can contribute to the image of a product, but it cannot sustain an image if the product itself is not worthy of it. This matrix looks at product/image differentiation and price differentiation, from the viewpoint of strategy formulation.

Product/image differentiation

		High	Low
Price differentiation	High	4	3
	Low	1	2

Instructions

On this matrix your products are positioned according to how they rate with competing products in terms of image differentiation and price differentiation.

Box 1   Products in this box have a good image and are significantly better than or different from other products in the same category. Yet they are on sale at a low price! This doesn't make much sense as a commercial policy. A better product at a lower price may well cause consumers to assume that there is no difference between this and other products. Why give your profit margin away unnecessarily? It only makes sense as a strategy if you have determined to enter the 'high differentiation/low costs' box of matrix 8 (box 2).

Box 2   Companies with products in this box get all they deserve. They really are commodity products and can't, therefore, expect to get anything other than low prices.

Box 3   Products in this box are what are often called 'pimply little me-toos', like those in box 2. The difference here is that they command a high price! The only possible explanation for this situation is either that consumers haven't found out yet (but inevitably, they soon will), or that the commodity in question is in short supply. Again, this is a situation which is unlikely to last for long.

Box 4   The best box of all. Here, products that have a high product or image differentiation also command a relatively high price. This is normally the 'branded' products box. They should be supported as long as possible with appropriate expenditure on R&D and/or promotion.

70 Discount structure (1)

The purpose of this matrix and the next two matrices is to start you thinking about whether, when and how, discounts should be given.

Level of competition

	Low	High
Old	1	2
New	3	4

Age of product/service

Box 1 Your product/service has been around for some time now, but there are not that many competitors. A decision about giving a price discount is not likely to be a necessity, but more of a strategic decision regarding particular customers, or competitors.

Box 2 The chances are that to make impact in this box you will have to differentiate your product/service in some way. A 'package' involving a discount might help in this respect.

Box 3 Customers should be fighting to get their hands on this product/service. To give a discount in these circumstances is to throw away profits, unless, of course, there isn't much demand.

Box 4 Much the same argument as for box 2 applies here, but if the market is showing high growth, think twice before opting for a price discount, unless your clear strategy is to go for market share growth.

71 Discount structure (2)

The use of discounts ought to provide you with some strategic advantage, rather than just being a blind adherence to custom and practice. For many companies, the prompt settlement of accounts (and the subsequent effect on cash flow) is a prime concern in terms of customer rating. This matrix explores how a discount policy might be established with this criterion in mind.

Settlement of accounts

	Early	Late
High	1	2
Low	3	4

Volume of orders

Instructions

Position all of your customers (or at least the major ones) on the matrix, having first decided what constitutes early and late settlement of accounts, and high and low orders, for your particular business.

Box 1 Nice customers to have, these! It could be argued that a price discount would not necessarily improve volume sales, nor encourage an early settlement of bills. So why do it? Explore the whole customer package to check if it is easier to provide other benefits, such as, for example, different bulk packaging.

Box 2 A discount to encourage an earlier settlement of bills would be worth considering here. The advantages of improving cash flow might well justify such a step.

Box 3 Not much to worry about here, except to consider if there is any inducement which would encourage orders of a higher volume.

Box 4 Who needs customers like these? See if you can get them paying on a pro-forma basis, or even charge extra for small orders.

72　Price and product surround

When customers purchase a product, they are in fact buying a 'bundle' of benefits which they perceive as satisfying their particular needs and wants. While the functional performance of the product is at the heart of the buying decision, many other factors are taken into account, such as price, appearance, guarantees, delivery, after-sales service, and so on. These are known as the product surround.

It has been estimated that while the core product incurs 80 per cent of the costs, it only makes 20 per cent of the impact on the customer. Conversely, the product surround can incur 20 per cent of the costs, but makes 80 per cent of the impact.

This matrix explores the factors which go to make up the product surround, and their relative value to customers, i.e. how much customers are prepared to pay to receive the additional benefits.

Read the instructions then complete the following matrix.

Elements of the product surround (example)	Extent to which customers will pay extra for a specific element of the product surround							
Quality								
Exclusiveness								
Design								
Availability								
Fast repair service								
Packaging								
Simplicity to use								
Training provided								
Customization								
Easier administration								
Credit facilities								
Etc								

Base　　　x　　　2x　　　3x　　　4x　　　5x　　　6x　　　7x　　　8x

Instructions

Step 1 Construct a matrix, with all the elements of your product surround listed down the vertical axis.

Step 2 Establish values for the base price and the incremental unit x (it might be pence, pounds, or hundreds of pounds).

Step 3 Consider each element of the product surround in turn and assess how much this is worth in the customer's eyes. The assessment could be made very subjectively, in which case the results might be very suspect. Having established a value, say it was 3x, shade in the horizontal row up to the 3x vertical line.

Step 4 When the matrix is completed, add up the total units of x above the base price. Now consider the implications of charging the base price plus the total x figures, taking into account,

- your overall objectives
- your competitive position

The best way is to carry out research with actual customers. Although this can be costly, a simple method of getting customer feedback is as follows:

- Present them with a list of the elements of the product surround.
- Ask them to cross out the element they would miss *least*, and give their reasoning.
- Next, the least valuable element is removed from the shortened list, as above, and this process is repeated until only one item remains. Clearly, this one item is the most valuable to the customer. Try to assess its value in money terms.
- Study the information you have collected and translate the customer's relative preferences into monetary values.

7 Advertising and promotion

73 Product life cycle and promotion

This matrix describes the different kinds of promotional effort that should be applied at different levels of market growth.

Promotional activity

	High	Low
High	4	3
Low	1	2

Market growth

Box 1 In this box, the market is either static or growing slowly, yet promotional activity is high. If a new product launch is involved, it can often make a lot of sense to spend quite heavily on promotion, particularly on advertising, in order to make the target market aware of the new product's existence. In such a case, looking for a quick profit can be the wrong thing to do, as profits will accrue after the product becomes better known and more frequently bought. On the other hand, if the market for a particular product is mature, i.e. there is little or no market growth, spending heavily on promotion can be a waste of money. In such a case, it is recommended that only sufficient promotional expenditure is incurred to retain market share.

Box 2 The very opposite of the advice given in respect of box 1 above applies here. In other words, the decision is generally correct if the market is mature and generally incorrect in the case of a 'new' product.

Box 3 Here, the market is growing rapidly, yet little effort is devoted to promotion. Generally speaking, the only circumstances in which this makes sense are in market conditions of product supply shortage, or if a company has deliberately decided to minimize its promotional spend in order to maximize its profitability in a high growth market. Beware, however, such short termism generally leads to long-term disaster as other companies outpace you and enjoy lower cost bases.

Box 4 Generally speaking, a high promotional effort in a high growth market will be the right decision, but see boxes 1, 2, and 3 above for exceptions.

74   When to use advertising and personal selling (1)

This matrix considers the appropriateness of using one-way communication (advertising), or two-way communication (sales force), when having to communicate messages of varying degrees of complexity.

Communication

	Advertising (one way)	Sales force (two way)
High	1	2
Low	3	4

Complexity of communication

Box 1   If you are using a one way communication process to convey complex information, then your chances of success will be extremely limited. Your best options would be:

- switch to a two-way communication process, by using a face-to-face approach with your customers, or
- try to simplify the message you are trying to put over.

Box 2   Here, the chances of success are much higher. Face-to-face communication enables your representative(s) to respond to the customer and phrase your proposition in a way which makes sense, taking into account the customer's particular circumstances.

Box 3   Again, a good match. Advertising is a good way to communicate simple messages to a wide audience. Clearly, to use an expensive resource like the sales force in such a situation would be a costly over-kill.

Box 4   Talking of costly over-kills . . . ! Some serious thinking has to be done here. Your main options would be:

- consider using indirect methods of communicating to your customers, or
- perhaps switch to telephone sales, rather than actual sales visits.

75 When to use advertising and personal selling (2)

This matrix is designed to help in making the decision about whether or not it is better to use the sales force, or advertising, to influence customer behaviour.

Complexity of product/service

	Low	High
High	1	2
Low	3	4

Commercial uncertainty surrounding purchase

Instructions

On this matrix, you plot products (or services) against the parameters shown. How you interpret low and high will be a reflection of the nature of your business.

Box 1 While the product/service is relatively simple, the commercial uncertainty surrounding the purchase is high. Probably the best strategy to use in these circumstances is:

- use face-to-face selling to build a persuasive case. The sales contact time need not be too long
- use indirect communications as a follow up to provide reassurance and on-going support

Box 2 Here is a role for the sales force, with back-up promotional material. The sales contact time in these circumstances might extend over several visits, as well as requiring some after-sales calls.

Box 3 Much of the communication problems in this box can be solved by indirect materials. To use face-to-face methods would be extremely costly.

Box 4 Again, face-to-face communication will be required, unless something can be done to reduce the complexity of the product/service.

76 Company image development

Several other matrices have referred to image, in the context of influencing the buying decision, or differentiating the product or company from its competitors. This particular matrix focuses attention on the topic of image development itself.

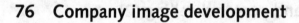

Current image

	Poor	Good
High	1	4
Low	2	3

Time/resources allocated to image development

Instructions

Place your company in the box which you believe most accurately reflects your current situation.

Box 1 Here, you see your current image as poor, and yet you are putting considerable resources into image development. Clearly, something is going wrong. Six possibilities spring to mind:

- you really are a grotty company and no amount of cosmetic tampering can hide this fact!
- the industry of which you are part has a poor image and unfortunately you are tarred with this brush (see the next matrix)
- the company is unclear what image it wants to project
- those responsible for image development are incompetent
- what you call a high allocation of resources is still inadequate for the task
- you have recognized that you have a poor image and are rightly trying to put it right

Box 2 You are getting exactly what you deserve. Presumably, not having a positive image doesn't worry you.

Box 3 You have discovered a magic formula which could make you a fortune, if you could sell it. Whatever it is, keep doing it.

Box 4   On the surface, you are getting a pay-off for your investment in image development. What you might care to do, is to evaluate which activities are contributing most to the cause. Having cultivated a good image, perhaps you can now be more selective in the ways that you maintain it.

77 Industry image

The purpose of this matrix is to put the issue of company image into the context of the image of its industry as a whole.

Clearly, this matrix, dealing as it does with imagery, is going to be somewhat subjective. Nevertheless, image is important and some companies spend fortunes attempting to improve how they are perceived by customers, the local community, employees, or indeed, any important group of stakeholders.

You will have to use your judgement regarding how you rate the image of your industry. In terms of how you rate your own image, you might decide that you are perceived differently by different customer groups. In that sense you will have more than one image. If these images are significantly different, it will be worth plotting each of them on the matrix.

Industry image

	Poor	Good
Good	1	2
Poor	4	3

Our image

Box 1 Well done, somehow you have managed to detach yourself from the poor image created by your industry. This should certainly give you some differential advantages over your competitors.

Box 2 This is really only par for the course. What you might need to aim for is an even better image, if you are to distance yourself from the masses.

Box 3 Companies in this box must have masochistic tendencies. To put oneself at such an obvious disadvantage is, to say the least, eccentric behaviour.

Box 4 This might not be as bad as it might look at first sight. If an industry has a poor image, an individual company can spend a fortune on image development and achieve nothing. In such circumstances, the best the company might do is to work to achieve an image which is as good as, or better, than its main competitors.

78 Types of sales promotion

It has to be remembered that a sales promotion is a short-term problem-solving activity, designed to get customers to behave more in line with the economic interests of the company. Typical tasks for sales promotion are moving slow stock; counteracting competitor activity; encouraging repeat purchase; securing marginal customers; getting bills paid on time; inducing trial purchase, and so on. From this it can be seen that sales promotion is not necessarily concerned with sales increases.

This matrix considers what promotional options are available.

	Nature of promotions		
	Money	Goods	Services
Consumers	1	2	3
Target market Channels	4	5	6
Sales force	7	8	9

Box 1 Here, the promotion is aimed at consumers, in the nature of financial inducements. Such promotions could include price reductions; coupons; vouchers; money prize competitions, and any money-equivalent inducements.

Box 2 Here, the emphasis switches to providing goods. These types of promotions could include free gifts; trade-in offers; premium offers e.g. 3 and 2; stamps; vouchers or coupons for goods; competitions, with goods as prizes.

Box 3 Promotions including services to consumers could include guarantees; group participation events; special exhibitions or displays; coupons or vouchers for services; a free trial; admission to events; competitions with service prizes.

Box 4 Here, the promotion is focused not on the consumer, but on the channel intermediary, such as distributors or retailers. Promotions concentrating on money could include dealer loaders; loyalty bonus incentives; full-range buying; extended credit; delayed invoicing; sale or return facilities; coupons; vouchers; competitions.

Box 5 Promotions of goods for trade intermediaries could include free gifts; trial offers; trade-ins; premium offers e.g. for every 12 crates, 1 extra crate free; coupons; vouchers and competitions.

Box 6 The provision of services to trade intermediaries could include free consultancy; staff training; demonstrations; special exhibitions and displays; risk-reduction schemes; reciprocal trading agreements; coupons; vouchers and competitions.

Box 7 At times, it can be useful to give one's own sales force added inducements. Monetary promotions could include special bonuses and commission; a points award system; coupons; vouchers; competitions with money prizes.

Box 8 Sales force promotions using goods could include free gifts; coupons or vouchers convertible to prizes; competitions with goods prizes.

Box 9 Sales force promotions using services could include free services; group participation events; event admission; competitions with services as prizes.

79 Advertising impact

For advertising to make impact it needs to be carefully targeted. This matrix explores some of the factors that contribute to such targeting.

Clarity of advertising objectives

	Ill-defined	Clear
Specific	1	2
Ill-defined	4	3

Target market segments

Instructions

Plot your most recent advertising (or campaigns) on this matrix, using a 10 point scale for each parameter. (10 points = clearly and specifically defined.)

Remember, however, that advertising cannot directly achieve sales (unless it is direct response advertising). To believe otherwise would be to assume that the product, its efficacy, packaging, price, customer service, the sales force, and so on had absolutely no impact at all, which is clearly nonsensical. Advertising then, can basically only create awareness or change attitudes – both of which can be measured quantitatively on a semantic scale.

Box 1 The impact of advertising here is not likely to be very high. All the good work that has been done by clearly identifying target market segments, is being dissipated by having woolly advertising objects.

Box 2 Here is a recipe for success which enables a campaign to be focused on target.

Box 3 The advertising objectives might be clear, but they may well be hitting the target market somewhat randomly. In this box, the company's market segments are ill-defined, so it may be costing too much to reach the right segments. Getting the segmentation right is the foundation on which successful marketing is built. By failing to do this, a company is merely trusting to luck.

Box 4 It was once said by a marketing executive that 'we probably waste 50 per cent of the money we spend on advertising . . . the problem is we don't know which 50 per cent it is.' Well! Companies in this box will do better than that . . . they will waste all the money they spend.

80 Targeting the message

This matrix focuses attention on the content of your advertising and asks you to consider how well you are targeting your message.

Basic message

	Standard benefits	Differential benefits

Strategic target

	Whole industry	1	2
	Defined segment	4	3

Box 1 This might be a safe strategy, if not earth-shattering. The reason for this is that for such a 'broad church' as a whole industry, it might be difficult to communicate differential benefits which would apply to everyone. Therefore, while standard benefits can provide an advertising platform, other promotional activity will be required to make impact on sub-groups of customers within the target industry.

Box 2 If you can achieve this, then you deserve success. However, for reasons given above, it is not always possible.

Box 3 As a marketer, if you are not emphasizing differential benefits to a defined target segment, then you are probably wasting much of your promotional spend. To be in box 3, then, should be your goal, and you are to be congratulated if you are already in it.

Box 4 Here, advertising may well be missing the boat and the potential business. The target audience is clearly defined, but all that they are getting is a message that could come from any of your competitors. So, you may be wasting your money. Beware.

81   Retail shelf allocation matrix

This matrix provides guidance about how retail shelf space might be best utilized in order to maximize profits.

Space responsiveness

	Low	Medium	High

Variable profit per square metre	High	4	3
	Medium		
	Low	1	2

Low   Medium   High

Instructions

Consider your product types in terms of the parameters of this matrix. Then plot them into the four boxes provided.

Clearly, any particular product type can, in turn, be subjected to deeper analysis by re-using the matrix for individual products or brands.

Box 1   Products in this box have a low variable profit per square metre and also do not respond well to additional space. Such products should be kept to a minimum and relegated to remote points of the store.

Box 2   Products in this box respond well to more shelf space but have low variable profit per square meter. Don't fill your store with these products!

Box 3   The best box of all, since these products enjoy high variable profit per square metre and respond well to additional space. Allocate as much space as possible to these products until the profit level begins to fall.

Box 4   Here, space responsiveness is poor, but variable profit per square metre is high. Work out the right amount of shelf space to maximize your profits.

82 Product support

The nature of a product (or service) largely dictates the nature of the type of support it requires. If the product is significantly different from its competitors, then it will pose different problems. If it requires more or less expertise to use, then that too needs to be taken into account. This matrix considers how these factors can combine.

Degrees of personalizaton
of product/service

	Differ- entiated	Undiffer- entiated
Differentiated	1	2
Undifferentiated	3	4

Expertise required

Box 1 With the product being highly personalized and requiring considerable expertise to use, the mode of product support will need to be in the nature of *consultancy*.

Box 2 Here, the product has a wider application, in that it is less personalized. However, it still requires special expertise, and so the mode of support will tend to be in the form of a *specialist/technician*.

Box 3 In this box, the level of expertise is much reduced, but there is still a high degree of personalization. This suggests that product support might be provided by specially selected and trained *agents*.

Box 4 Here, the situation is relatively straightforward and product support can probably be handled by *retailers and traders*.

83 Should we exhibit?

To have a stand at an exhibition can be an expensive business. Sometimes, it does not justify the cost and effort that went into it. This matrix provides a framework for deciding whether or not exhibiting will be successful.

Before deciding to exhibit at any particular exhibition, consider where it would fit on this matrix.

Analysis of attendance population

	Not favourable	Favourable
Many	1	2
Few	3	4

Likely number of competitors exhibiting

Box 1 This exhibition does not have the right target population, yet for some reason, many of your competitors will be there. The short answer is to let them waste their time while you usefully use yours . . . elsewhere. If you are paranoid about them stealing a march on you (which doesn't look very likely), then instead of taking a stand, why not just sponsor something associated with the exhibition to keep your name visible?

Box 2 The chances are that it will be worthwhile exhibiting here, but because of the competition, you will have to get 'market penetration.' In practical terms this means trying to get a stand in a strategic position in the exhibition hall, and making sure it is attention-grabbing.

Box 3 Again, this is not an exhibition worth bothering about. The fact that there are few competitors, does not make it all that attractive, bearing in mind the composition of the attendance population.

Box 4 This type of exhibition offers you the greatest prospects of success.

84   Exhibition evaluation

This matrix provides a framework against which the success of 'exhibiting' can be evaluated.

Number of enquiries

		Below target	Above target
Resulting sales	Above target	1	2
	Below target	3	4

Box 1   Here you received fewer enquiries than you targeted for, yet these were converted to a high level of sales. There are many positives from this situation:

- your enquiries must have been genuine
- your sales conversion rate is impressive
- your customer 'package' must be very competitive

However, perhaps your stand design did not make the necessary impact, or perhaps the way it was manned let some potential enquiries slip away.

Box 2   You seem to be managing exhibitions in a very productive way.

Box 3   Something is going badly wrong here. You will need to reappraise many things:

- were you at the right exhibition? (see matrix 83)
- was your stand strategically positioned?
- was your stand well-designed and customer friendly?
- were your exhibition staff suitably trained?
- were there enough staff manning your stand?
- how were follow-up sales visits arranged?
- who did them?
- how skilled were the sales staff?
- how competitive is your customer package?

Box 4   Here, nothing seems to be wrong with your stand. The only problem is that you were either getting the wrong kind of enquiries (black mark on your stand staff), or your follow-up procedure is inadequate (see points in box 3)

8 Distribution and customer service

85 Product life cycle/customer service

This matrix illustrates how customer service levels need to change as a product goes through its life cycle.

Customer service levels

	High	Low
High	4	3
Low	1	2

Market growth

Box 1 Shows a company operating in a low market growth situation and providing high customer service levels. If it's an embryonic market, this can be a good investment in building market loyalty, but remember, a high level of customer service costs money, so if it's a mature or declining market, think carefully about whether you are over-servicing your customers.

Box 2 The same logic applies here as in box 1. If it's an embryonic market, poor service will hardly inspire confidence. On the other hand, in a mature/declining market, lower levels of service (but not inadequate levels) will probably save you money without losing customers.

Box 3 This box shows low service levels in a high-growth market. This could either be due to supply shortage or to poor management. In the former case, while you can probably get away with it in the short term, remember that customers have long memories and have a habit of dropping you once they have a choice, so if it is due to supply shortage, make sure you service well those customers you want to keep in the long term.

Box 4 Generally speaking, it makes a lot of sense to give good service in a growth market. Customers expect and achieve good service. As in box 3, if there is a shortage, the best thing to do is to select those customers in segments you want to deal with in the long term, and give them good service in preference to others.

86 Customer service management

Customer service can be expensive to provide, so the company needs to be sure that its investment in this area provides the best possible pay-off in terms of customer satisfaction, as well as giving it a competitive edge. This matrix provides a management indicator about whether or not the company is addressing the right issues.

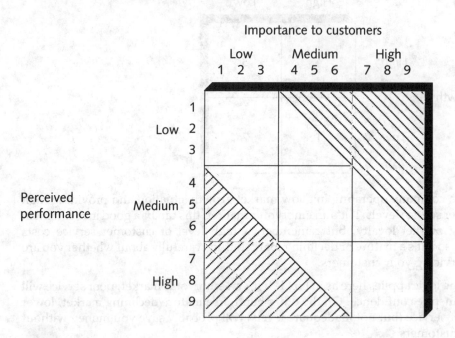

Instructions

Step 1 Make a list of all the customer service factors pertinent to your business e.g. on time delivery, packaging, regular servicing etc.

Step 2 Grade each of these low, medium or high according to their importance to the customer. (If you want more accuracy, use the 9 point scale.)

Step 3 Similarly, grade each element of customer service in terms of its perceived performance.

Step 4 Plot each element of customer service on the matrix, using the co-ordinates established in steps 2 and 3. Use a number, or code letter, to identify each item of customer service on the matrix.

Step 5   Compare the positioning of the elements of customer service against this key:

= under-performance area, corrective action is required

= target area customer service is in focus

= over-kill area, you are working too hard at the unimportant things, take corrective action

87 Inventory

In planning customer service levels it is important to consider the strategic importance of specific market segments, and the consequences of failing to meet their expectations. This matrix is designed to explore those issues.

Strategic importance of customer segment

	Low	High
High	2	3
Low	1	4

Risk of a stock-out situation

Instructions

On this matrix, you will need to consider your market segments in terms of their importance (horizontal axis), and the vulnerability of their supplies from you (vertical axis).

Box 1   Here, the risk of stock-out is low, as is the strategic importance of these customers. It is not really a problem area, except that inventory levels might be too high and savings could be made.

Box 2   Clearly, the customer service requirement levels are not unduly pressing here. Stock-outs are embarrassments rather than disasters.

Box 3   Here is the *'headache'* box. It is the area where inventory management is most critical. All efforts should be focused on this box, even at the expense of others.

Box 4   Since the risk of stock-out is low, the situation needs to be monitored, but a watching brief might be all that is required.

88 Physical distribution

This matrix looks at providing delivery service levels over wide geographical areas.

Location of customer

	Near	Far
High	1	2
Low	3	4

Service level required

Box 1 Here, we have customers near to us that require high service levels, when it comes to deliveries. Distribution straight from the plant would seem the best option here.

Box 2 The same high standards of delivery are required, but now the customers are distanced from us. In these circumstances it would make sense to distribute from local depots, or from local distributors who have appropriate storage facilities. Small orders can be sent via express couriers.

Box 3 Local deliveries can be made, or customers could be encouraged to collect.

Box 4 Distribution could be through carrier networks, or through conventional distribution channels.

89 Stock levels

Stock levels have to be related to demand forecasts, otherwise the expense involved in holding stock can be punitive. This matrix merely asks you to ensure that the two are in harmony.

Stocking level

	Low	High
High	1	2
Low	3	4

Forecast demand

Box 1 Unless your production plant can make the product at the forecast rate, there will be trouble. There is no flexibility in the system, because stocks are minimal.

Box 2 Let's hope the forecasts were accurate, otherwise there will be an awful lot of capital tied up in stocks. The logistics of production and storage have to be managed very astutely in this box.

Box 3 Probably you have got it about right in this box.

Box 4 There is an expensive mismatch here. You are holding a lot of stock for a low forecast demand. What are you going to do about it? See matrix 87, to help your thinking.

90 Distribution – strategic choice of outlets

As companies try to differentiate themselves from their competitors, distribution becomes one element in the marketing mix which offers some interesting options. This matrix illustrates the strategic choices open to a company by changing either the nature of its outlets, or the emphasis of the offer e.g. product, quality, convenience, service, price etc.

Outlet type

	Existing	New
Existing	1	2
New	3	4

Offer type

Box 1 Here, the distribution strategy is to maintain the status quo and stay with the existing outlets and offer type. However, if this choice is coming under pressure because of increased competitor activity, it might be appropriate to move to another box.

Box 2 Here, the choice is to keep the offer type the same, but to use new outlets. This could mean, for example, instead of dealing through wholesalers, going direct to retailers. Equally, it might mean leaving the home market and exporting through foreign agents.

Box 3 In this box the existing outlets are retained, but the offer is completely revamped. This could mean switching the emphasis from 'cheap and cheerful' to 'quality and high value'. It could mean introducing a whole new product range.

However, if this option is chosen, careful consideration would have to be made that the existing outlets were in fact compatible with the new offer. For example, is their image appropriate? Do they have the capability to handle the new offer? If they are found to be wanting then box 4 might be a better choice.

Box 4 Here, the strategic choice is to go for new outlets and a new offer. This type of solution has been adopted by Sainsbury's, when they diversified out of their traditional grocery range into the DIY market, setting up a new chain of super-stores.

At another level it could involve a company setting up a mail-order facility for a new product type, or opening a shop in the high street.

91 Selecting intermediaries

Selecting intermediaries is, for most businesses, the most crucial marketing decision that has to be made, yet often only casual methods are used in the selection process. This matrix should be used to improve this crucial decision-making process.

Subjective factors

	Low	Favourable
	1	10

	Low	Favourable
10 Many	1	2
1 Few	3	4

Objective factors

Instructions

Step 1 Consider the relevant objective factors that would influence your choice when selecting a channel intermediary. Here are some possible examples:

- location (market place)
- communication (ease of contacting)
- facilities/capacity
- track record/experience
- technical competence
- credit rating
- size of salesforce
- number of contacts
- exclusivity (i.e. the extent the intermediary is involved with other principals)
- common language
- other factors

Step 2 List those factors that would be particularly appropriate for your business.

Step 3 Allocate a points score of 1–10 against each item on your list (10 is high), regarding the extent to which the intermediary meets your requirements.

Step 4 Allocate a weighting factor for each item on the list (see matrix 6 for instructions about producing weighting scores).

Step 5 Repeat all the above steps, but this time focusing on subjective factors, such as:

- image
- degree of confidence, or trust generated etc.
- warmth in relationship
- quality of staff
- other factors

Step 6 Plot all potential intermediaries on the matrix, positioning each one according to the scores.

Box 1 Although this intermediary rates highly on the objective analysis, subjectively there is a low score. Ignore this intermediary. You must feel entirely comfortable about getting into a business relationship, and so you have to *feel* that it is going to be right.

Box 2 Any that fall into this box hold every prospect of being the right ones for you.

Box 3 Don't waste time with these people.

Box 4 The chances are that these will not be suitable intermediaries, but those with marginal scores on the objective scale might be worth cultivating. If you need representation in their areas, then it might pay you to invest in a modest way to improve their 'objectivity' rating. But don't let your head be over-ruled by your heart.

92 Frequency of intermediary visits

Clearly, one way of resolving the question about how frequently to call on your distributors or agents would be to use a matrix like number 54. This matrix proposes an alternative approach which is based on the proposition that your intermediaries should be seen as being 'on your team', not as part of the 'opposition'.

		We believe we communicate		
		Too little	About right	Too frequently
	Too frequently	3	6	9
Intermediary believes we communicate	About right	2	5	8
	Too little	1	4	7

Instructions

Consider each intermediary in turn and consider the frequency of your contacts with them, and your understanding of what they think of the current arrangements. If you are not sure of their opinion, try asking. You might get some surprises.

Box 1 For whatever reasons, both of you believe you ought to communicate more. In these circumstances, it would seem stupid not to do so.

Box 2 He/she is quite happy with the situation, but you have doubts. Unless things are going wrong, try to live with this arrangement.

Box 3 Clearly, what is too little for you, is much too much for the recipient. Could it be that you have an insatiable curiosity to know what is going on? Or can you not delegate?

Box 4 Try to find out why the intermediary wants to see you more frequently. Perhaps he is experiencing more problems than you imagine.

Box 5 You seem to have contact schedules at about the right frequency.

Box 6   Here, you need to find out why you are seen as providing an 'over-kill' in communications. As with box 3, perhaps you have difficulty letting the intermediary get on with the job.

Box 7   This intermediary seems to be having trouble and clearly needs more support. You will need to revise your communication strategy with them.

Box 8   Nothing much to worry about here. Try checking out what reactions there could be if you reduced communications, or more pertinently, one or two aspects of your communications.

Box 9   There is no reason whatsoever to be in this position. Take corrective action immediately.

93 Channel intermediary communication

Everybody nods vigorously in agreement whenever the importance of having good communications with distributors or agents is discussed. However, it has been shown, time and time again, that good communications are in fact something of a rarity. This matrix helps to explain why.

Reasons for principal's contact

	Something has gone wrong	Planned and agreed
Admonishment	1	2
Consulting, problem solving	3	4

Mode of meeting

Box 1　This box typifies the communication pattern that frequently occurs. Certainly, overseas agents say that the only times they see representatives of the supplying company is when things have gone wrong. If things are going well . . . a resounding silence! Clearly, meetings taking place in this context are not going to be very motivating, and the types of relationship they engender are not likely to form the basis of a productive collaboration.

Box 2　This is even worse, if 'butt kicking' meetings are actually planned on a regular basis. We suggest that you reappraise the way you select your intermediaries.

Box 3　Even though at best this will be a rescue operation, it has the advantage over the above two boxes in that it doesn't set out to apportion blame, but to solve a problem.

Box 4　This appears to be the most productive mode of communications. The regular two way consultation process enables problems to be 'nipped in the bud'. Moreover, such meetings will encourage a greater level of openness and trust between both parties. It is these ingredients which are essential to a recipe for success.

94   Intermediaries' performance

This matrix is designed to prompt ways to assess and improve the performance of channel intermediaries.

Clarity of role

	Low	High
High	1	2
Low	3	4

Clarity of operational procedures

Box 1   In this box the intermediary has a good grasp of all the operating procedures but is underperforming because there is confusion regarding the role he/she is expected to play.

Box 2   Your best performers ought to be located in this box and it is easy to see why. They are clear about both their role and the operating procedures.

Box 3   In this box, performance is hampered by a communications breakdown. There is a huge training/educational programme required by these intermediaries if they are to reach acceptable performance levels.

Box 4   These intermediaries are clear about their role, but limit their effectiveness by being uncertain about the operational procedures they should be following.

9 Exporting

95 Reasons for exporting

It can be shown that companies get involved in exporting for a wide variety of reasons. Sometimes the stimulus for exporting comes from within the company, sometimes it is an external factor which triggers the action. Similarly, some companies take a very pro-active stance, while others are merely passive exporters.

It is important for an organization to understand how and why they are exporting, because their 'first steps' can colour how their export marketing is subsequently developed, and perhaps impose meaningless constraints.

Stimulus for exporting

	Internal	External
Pro-active	1	2
Re-active	3	4

Company stance

Box 1 This box would appear to contain the best motives for exporting. Clearly there is a management initiative to make things happen and it is likely that this strategic thinking is influenced by considerations about:

- future growth and profit goals
- economies of scale
- exploiting technical competence/product advantages
- not imposing artificial geographical constraints on the definition of market segments.

Box 2 Here the company is still pro-active but the stimulus for exporting is external in origin, e.g. a market opportunity appears, or external 'change agent', such as a chamber of commerce, or trade association provides the vital spark.

Box 3 Here the motives for exporting will be more 'defensive' in nature. For example:

- to spread risks
- to use excess capacity
- to reduce the effect of seasonal sales patterns in the home market
- in response to a stagnant or declining home market

Box 4 This could almost be described as 'exporting by accident', yet surprisingly many companies, particularly small ones start exploiting by just reacting to external stimuli. Invariably, what happens is, they receive unsolicited orders from abroad.

96   International competitiveness

In order to be successful internationally, the company must be able to match the standards of performance of its competitors, as well as seeking to win a sustainable strategic advantage over them.

However, not all companies have the necessary 'global mindset'. Instead of thinking in terms of international competitive performance benchmarks, managers stay fixed on the traditional, domestic ones. Equally, although the management ought to design a strategy first and then implement it by using the appropriate tactics, many companies appear to lack an overall strategy. Instead, they react to situations by modifying their short-term tactical recipe.

This matrix illustrates how all these factors combine.

Box 1   Most successful international companies operate in this box. They 'think' globally in terms of standards of competitiveness and follow well-conceived strategies.

Box 2   Companies in this box might aspire to international greatness and recognize what is required to be competitive. However, they will always be held back by not having a coherent strategy which seeks to give them a sustainable competitive advantage.

Box 3   Many companies successful in domestic markets might be found in this box. However, while there is no conceptual difference between strategic management for domestic or international companies, these companies will find themselves working to the wrong competitive standards if they trade globally.

Box 4   Companies in this box will never be successful in international markets (or for that matter in domestic ones). Their over-concern for short-term tactical solutions, geared to domestic benchmarks, is doomed to fail.

97 Selecting export markets (1)

It is something of a misnomer to talk of selecting export markets, because in reality it is a process of rejecting them by using various screening processes.

This matrix is designed to give you an opportunity of reducing a large number of possible world markets down to a small number of potentially suitable ones.

Broad factors Market attractiveness	Possible export market						
(Example)	1	2	3	4	5	6	7
Prospects for growth							
Similar culture							
Same language							
Political stability							
Sound economy							
Accessibility							
Distribution infrastructure							
Contacts							
Affinity with country/people							
Demography							
Technical sophistication							
Total							

Instructions

Step 1 Make a list of the broad issues which would make an export market attractive for your business. The matrix above provides an example of this.

Step 2 Pick out the five factors which are of the greatest significance.

Step 3 Give each of these a weighting which reflects their relative value.

Step 4 Across the horizontal axis of the matrix, enter possible export markets, in positions 1 to 7.

Step 5 Take export market number 1 and score how it rates (between 1–10 points) against the critical factors. Multiply each score by the appropriate weighting and enter on the matrix. Finally add all the weighted scores and enter the sum in the total box.

Step 6 Repeat this process for all other possible export markets.

Step 7 Those markets with the highest total scores will be those worth examining in more detail.

98 Selecting export markets (2)

Following on from the previous matrix, the export market rejection process is refined still further.

Barriers to entry

	Few	Many
High	Success box	Possible
Low	Long shot	Eliminate

Financial assessment

Instructions

The previous matrix should have helped you to eliminate a lot of unsuitable export markets, without having to conduct lengthy research.

Those few markets that passed the first screening will now have to be analysed in more depth.

Step 1 Consider your short list of markets and find out as much as you can about them in terms of barriers to entry.

Factors to consider might be legislation, tariffs, high competition, unfavourable exchange rates, preferred trading arrangements, and so on.

Step 2 Weight and score each of these factors as in the previous matrix. Add up the total weighted scores for each of your short-listed export markets, and select only the top two or three.

Step 3 Taking this selection of markets with very few barriers to entry, study each market in detail and calculate the level of business you can expect to generate.

Step 4 Select and concentrate on the export market which has fewest barriers and which offers the highest prospects of success.

99 Background issues for exporters

The choice of an export market can be complicated by a number of issues regarding the socio-economic and political environment of the particular target country. The exporter must check all of these issues to ensure that they do not impose too much of a barrier to success. If they do, then regardless of other positive signals, the exporter would be wise to reconsider whether or not to go ahead.

This matrix introduces some of the issues which need to be taken into account. Clearly, not every box is going to be equally important for all exporters.

1 Values and attitudes	2 Politics	3 Education and technology
4 Culture	? (arrows radiating)	5 Economy
6 Language	7 Infra-structure	8 Law

Box 1 *Values and attitudes* can include, views about ownership, fashion, credit, work, wealth, change, new ideas, punctual deliveries, quality, choice, etc.

Box 2 *Politics* issues about the nature of the country's politics, ideology, stability, relationship with the outside world and the exporter's country in particular can all be important.

Box 3 *Education and technology* provide some measure of the sophistication of the country. For example, what is the literacy level, level of education in general, attitude to science and new ideas, level of industrialization, nature of power supply and public utilities etc.

Box 4 *Culture* looks at what are the philosophical systems, religions, taboos, rituals, history (e.g. was the country once a colony?), class structure, social groups, status systems and so on.

Box 5 *Economy* – is it buoyant or depressed, level of debt, banking system, currency exchange level, hard currency or soft etc ?

Box 6 *Language* – most common spoken language, secondary languages, written languages, degree of acceptance of foreign languages, mass media etc.

Box 7 *Infrastructure* can include issues which affect how goods can be distributed to customers e.g. transport systems, advertising, media, retail chain, communications, degree of urbanization etc.

Box 8 *Law* can involve law affecting trading in general in the target country, and also law relating to the product e.g. safety, product liability, guarantees, component materials, finishes, etc.

100 Phases of exporting

It can be shown that exporting evolves through a number of successive phases. At each phase there are a number of distinctly characteristic features regarding the exporter's motives, the way markets are selected, the mode of entry into the market, and the sort of problems that are commonly experienced.

How these combine is shown in the matrix below.

Evolutionary exporting phases

	Passive	Experimental	Expansive	Consolidated
Motives	• none • opportunism • short-term profit	• adjust for seasonality • use spare capacity	• management decision • sales growth • seize opportunities	• long-term profit
Market selection	• none • enquiries are unsolicited	• close export markets • using personal contacts	• near or distant markets • segmentation	• market concentration and specialization
Entry mode	• direct sales to customer	• use sales agents	• sales agents • set up own sales offices	• own sales offices
Problems	• no build up of experience • each new order is a 'problem', especially documentation	• selecting agent • adjusting to requirements of exporting	• managing the enterprise • building market share	• growth difficult to manage • co-ordination between markets

158

10 Glossary of terms

Glossary of marketing planning terms

Assumptions: the *major* assumptions on which the marketing plan is based.

Benefit: a perceived or stated relationship between a product feature and the need the feature is designed to satisfy. See also **Differential Advantage** and **Feature**.

Business plan: a plan commonly intermediate between a company's strategic plan and its annual marketing plan. The purpose of the business plan is to establish the broad, business objectives and strategies to be pursued by the business unit or centre over a time period of as many as five years. In this respect, business plans are similar to strategic plans which concern themselves with equally long time frames. Business plans are like strategic plans in one other respect – usually they deal with such strategic considerations as new product development, product acquisition, and new market development to achieve desired financial goals. Business plans also require extensive marketing input for their formulation and in this respect, they share characteristics in common with marketing plans. However, business plans generally do not include action programmes – a feature typical of marketing plans – but simply spell out intentions and directions. For example, if new product development was among the strategies to be pursued, this would be stated along with appropriate supporting rationale. However, the statement of this strategy would not be accompanied by a new product development plan.

Charter: a statement of the chief function or responsibility of an operating unit within an organization made up of several operating units. See also **Mission**.

Core strategy: a term used in marketing to denote the predominant elements of the marketing mix, selected by marketing management to achieve the optimum match between the benefits customers seek and those the product offers. This process of selection is sometimes referred to as 'making the differential advantage operational'.

Differential advantage: a benefit or cluster of benefits offered to a sizeable group of customers which they value (and are willing to pay for) and which they cannot obtain elsewhere. See also **Feature** and **Benefit**.

Distribution: a term used in marketing to refer to the means by which a product or service is made physically available to customers. Distribution encompasses such activities as warehousing, transportation, inventory control, order processing, etc. Because distribution is the means of increasing a product's availability, it is also a tool which can be used by marketing management to improve the match between benefits sought by customers and those offered by the organization.

Experience effect: it is a proven fact that most value-added cost components of a product decline steadily with experience and can be reduced significantly as the scale of operation increases. In turn this cost (and therefore price advantage) is a significant factor in increasing the company's market share.

Feature: a characteristic or property of a product or service such as reliability, price, convenience, safety and quality. These features may or may not satisfy customer needs. To the extent that they do, they can be translated into benefits. See also **Benefit** and **Differential advantage**.

Gap: in marketing terms, the difference between a product's present or projected performance and the level sought. Typically, the gaps in marketing management are those relating to return on investment, cash generation or use, return on sales and market share.

Gap analysis: the process of determining gaps between a product's present or projected performance and the level of performance sought. See also **Gap**.

Growth/share matrix: a term synonymous with 'product portfolio' which in essence is a means of displaying graphically the amount of 'experience' or market share a product has and comparing this share with the rate of growth of the relevant market segment. With the matrix, a manager can decide, for example, whether he or she should invest in getting more 'experience' – that is, fight for bigger market share – or perhaps get out of the market altogether. These choices are among a number of strategic alternatives available to the manager – strategic in the sense that they not only affect marketing strategy but determine use of capital within the organization. See also the **Experience effect**.

Marketing audit: a situational analysis of the company's current marketing capability. See also **Situational analysis**.

Marketing mix: 'tools' or means available to an organization to improve the match between benefits sought by customers and those offered by the organization so as to obtain a differential advantage. Among these tools are product price, promotion and distribution service. See also **Differential advantage**.

Marketing objectives: a statement of the targets or goals to be pursued and achieved within the period covered in the marketing plan. Depending on the scope and orientation of the plan – whether, for example, the plan is designed primarily to spell out short-term marketing intentions or to identify broad, business directions and needs – the objectives stated may encompass such important measures of business performance as profit, growth and market share.

Marketing objectives with respect to profit, market share, sales volume, market development or penetration and other, broader considerations are sometimes referred to as 'primary' marketing objectives. More commonly, they are referred to as 'strategic' or 'business' objectives since they pertain to the operation of the business as a whole. In turn, objectives set for specific marketing sub-functions or activities are referred to as 'programme' objectives to distinguish them from the broader, business or strategic objectives they are meant to serve.

Marketing plan: contains a mission statement, SWOT analysis assumption, marketing objectives, marketing strategies and programmes. Note that the objectives, strategies and policies are established for each level of the business.

Market segment: a group of actual or potential customers who can be expected to respond in approximately the same way to a given offer; a finer, more detailed breakdown of a market.

Market segmentation: a critical aspect of marketing planning and one designed to convert product differences into a cost differential that can be maintained over the product's life cycle. See also **Product life cycle**.

Market share: the per cent of the market represented by a firm's sales in relation to total sales. Some marketing theorists argue that the term is misleading since it suggests that the dimensions of the market are known and assumes that the size of the market is represented by the amount of goods sold in it. All that is known, these theorists point out and correctly, is the volume sold – in actuality, the market may be considerably larger.

Mission: a definite task with which one is charged – the chief function of an institution or organization. In essence it is a vision of what the company is or is striving to become. The basic issue is 'What is our business and what should it be?' In marketing planning, the mission statement is the starting point in the planning process, since it sets the broad parameters within which marketing objectives are established, strategies developed, and programmes implemented. Some companies, usually those with several operating units or divisions make a distinction between 'mission' and 'charter'. In these instances, the term mission, is used to denote the broader purpose of the organization as reflected in corporate policies or assigned by the senior management of the company. The term, charter, in comparison, is used to denote the purpose or reason for being of individual units with prime responsibility for a specific functional or product-market area.

Objective: a statement or description of a desired, future result that cannot be predicted in advance but which is believed, by those setting the objective, to be achievable through their efforts within a given time period; a quantitative target or goal to be achieved in the future through one's efforts, which can also be used to measure performance. To be of value, objectives should be specific in time and scope and attainable given the financial, technical and human resources available. According to this definition, general statements of hopes or desire are not true 'objectives'. See also **Marketing objectives**.

Planning: the process of pre-determining a course or courses of action based on assumptions about future conditions or trends which can be imagined but not predicted with any certainty.

Policies: guidelines adopted in implementing the strategies selected. In essence, a policy is a summary statement of objectives and strategies.

Positioning: the process of selecting, delineating and matching the segment of the market with which a product will be most compatible.

Product: a term used in marketing to denote not only the product itself – its inherent properties and characteristics – but also service, availability, price, and other factors which may be as important in differentiating the product from those of competitors as the inherent characteristics of the product itself. See also **Marketing mix**.

Product life cycle: a term used in marketing to refer to the pattern of growth and decline in sales revenue of a product over time. This pattern is typically divided into stages – introduction, growth, maturity, saturation and decline. With time, competition among firms tends to reduce all products in the market to commodities – products which are only marginally differentiable from each other with the result that pioneering companies – those first to enter the market – face the choice of becoming limited volume, high-priced, high-cost speciality producers or high-volume, low-cost producers of standard products.

Product portfolio: a theory about the alternative uses of capital by business organizations formulated originally by Bruce Henderson of the Boston Consulting Group, a leading firm in the area of corporate strategy consulting. This theory or approach to marketing strategy formulation has gained wide acceptance among managers of diversified companies, who were first attracted by the intuitively appealing notion that long-run corporate performance is more than the sum of the contributions of individual profit centres or product strategies. Other factors which account for the theory's appeal are its usefulnes in developing specific marketing strategies designed to achieve a balanced mix of products that will produce maximum return from scarce cash and managerial resources; and the fact that the theory employs a simple matrix representation useful in portraying and communicating a product's position in the market place. See also **Growth/share matrix**.

Programme: a term used in marketing planning to denote the steps or tasks to be undertaken by marketing, field sales and other functions within an organization to implement the chosen strategies and to accomplish the objectives set forth in the marketing plan. Typically, descriptions of programmes include a statement of objectives as well as a definition of the persons or units responsible and a schedule for completion of the steps or tasks for which the person or unit is responsible. See also **Strategy statement** and **Marketing objectives**.

Relative market share: a firm's share of the market relative to its largest competitor. See also **Market share**.

Resources: broadly speaking, anyone or anything through which something is produced or accomplished; in marketing planning, a term used to denote the unique capabilities or skills that an organization brings to a market or business problem or opportunity.

Situational analysis: the second step in the marketing planning process (the first being the definition of mission), and reviews the business environment at large (with particular attention to economic, market and competitive aspects) as well as the company's own internal operation. The purpose of the situational analysis is to identify marketing problems and opportunities, both those stemming from the organization's internal strengths and limitations, and those external to the organization and caused by changes in economic conditions and trends, competition, customer expectations, industry relations, government regulations and, increasingly, social perceptions and trends. The output of the full analysis is summarized in key point form under the heading SWOT (strengths, weaknesses, opportunities and threats) analysis; this summary then becomes part of the marketing plan. The outcome of the situational analysis includes a set of assumptions about future conditions as well as an estimate or forecast of potential market demand during the period covered by the marketing plan. Based on these estimates and assumptions, marketing objectives are established and strategies and programmes formulated.

Strategy statement: a description of the broad course of action to be taken to achieve a specific marketing objective such as an increase in sales volume or a reduction in unit costs. The strategy statement is frequently referred to as the connecting link between marketing objectives and programmes – the actual concrete steps to be taken to achieve those objectives. See also **Programme**.

Target: something aimed at: a person or group of persons to be made the object of an action or actions intended, usually to bring about an effect or change in the person or group of persons, e.g., our target is the canned food segment of the market.

Index